KIDS ARE AMERICANS TOO

Also by
Bill O'Reilly

Culture Warrior

The O'Reilly Factor for Kids:
A Survival Guide for America's Families
(coauthored with Charles Flowers)

Those Who Trespass

Who's Looking Out for You?

The No Spin Zone: Confrontations with
the Powerful and Famous in America

The O'Reilly Factor:
The Good, the Bad, and the Completely
Ridiculous in American Life

WILLIAM MORROW *An Imprint of* HarperCollins*Publishers*

KIDS
ARE AMERICANS TOO

Bill O'Reilly
and Charles Flowers

HarperCollins books may be purchased for educational, business, or sales promotional use. For information please write: Special Markets Department, HarperCollins Publishers, 10 East 53rd Street, New York, NY 10022.

FIRST EDITION

Designed by Janet M. Evans

Library of Congress Cataloging-in-Publication Data has been applied for.

ISBN: 978-0-06-084676-3
ISBN-10: 0-06-084676-3

07 08 09 10 11 ID/RRD 10 9 8 7 6 5 4 3 2 1

This book is for Madeline and Spencer, who hopefully will develop into great Americans and improve their country. Your Dad Loves You.

—B.O'R.

For Sharon Canup, whose dry wit and good heart are missed, but essential to these pages.

—C.F.

CONTENTS

Acknowledgments ★ *xi*

Welcome ★ *xiii*

First Up ★ *xix*

1 How Can You Be a Good American? ★ *1*
Your Hero? ★ *5*

2 A Blast from the Past ★ *7*
Unintended Consequences ★ *9*

3 What Is Your Freedom All About? ★ *15*
Ask O'Reilly ★ *20*
Musical Interlude ★ *24*
Reality Check ★ *25*
Awesome Multiple-Choice Quiz No. 1 ★ *26*

4 Last Piece of the Rights Puzzle: Listen Up! ★ *29*
O'Reilly Swings ★ *33*
Are the Supremes Your Friends? ★ *35*
Porn Judgment? ★ *37*

5 Your Life in the School Daze ★ *45*
When Is a Knight Not a Knight? ★ *47*
Awesome Multiple-Choice Quiz No. 2 ★ *52*
On the Other Hand . . . ★ *54*
Musical Interlude ★ *56*
Ask O'Reilly ★ *58*
High Ideals? ★ *61*
Awesome Multiple-Choice Quiz No. 3 ★ *70*

6 **All in the Family ★** *73*

   Parents Under Attack? ★ 77

7 **Your Rights vs. Their Rights ★** *87*

   Prose and a Con? ★ 88

   Sticking Up for Others ★ 94

   Freedom of the Press? ★ 96

   Ask O'Reilly ★ 97

   Are Rights Always Good for You? ★ 99

8 **Gotta Keep Thinking About These Things ★** *103*

   Careful What You Ask For ★ 104

   Ask O'Reilly ★ 106

   Final Awesome Multiple-Choice Quiz ★ 110

Extra Credit ★ 113

Ask O'Reilly ★ 123

The Last Word ★ 125

Defense Savvy: A Brief Guide to Terms ★ 127

ACKNOWLEDGMENTS

Could not have been done without ace agent Eric Simonoff, purveyor of calm Makeda Wubneh, excellent editor Hope Innelli, and keeper of the domestic flame Maureen O'Reilly.

—B.O'R.

Long ago, Brainerd Junior High School teacher "Lassie" Munsey labored tirelessly against great odds to teach a raucous all-boy class about our rights. Hope this book gets it right, Miss Munsey.

—C.F.

WELCOME

Welcome to the real world.

That's right . . . The real deal: life in the United States of America, where you are a citizen. Millions all over the world would like to be in your sneakers . . . So together let's begin looking at the countless reasons why.

A QUICK BITE OF REALITY TV

SETTING: Friday Harbor, a quiet village on an island off the coast of Washington State. Boats, gulls, waves, breezes—you know the kind of thing.

SCENE: The modest home of single mother Carmen Dixon and her daughter Lacy, fourteen. Mom's home alone. The phone rings.

Mrs. Dixon: Hello?

Sheriff: Mrs. Dixon, this is Sheriff Cumming.

Mrs. Dixon: Is Lacy all right?

Sheriff: She's fine, ma'am, so far as I know. But she's got a boyfriend who may be in trouble.

Mrs. Dixon: I knew it. It's Oliver. He's too old for her. He's seventeen.

Sheriff: Well, I think he mugged an old lady downtown and ran off with her purse.

Mrs. Dixon: Lacy would never be involved in something like that.

Sheriff: Yes, ma'am. But maybe Oliver—you know how he is—would brag to her, and tell her what he did with the purse.

Mrs. Dixon: I see. Well, I'll do what I can.

Sheriff: Thanks.

Mrs. Dixon puts down the receiver just as her daughter walks in. The phone rings again.

Lacy: That's probably Oliver, Mom. I'll take it on the extension in my bedroom.

The girl walks into the next room. Her mother very quietly picks up the kitchen phone.

Oliver: (on telephone, laughing)—and then I took out the money and threw the old lady's purse into those weeds near the railroad crossing.

CUT.

Okay, this little slice of reality TV might not make the top ten, but it's all true. It happened, and so did a lot more than that, as you'll see. I think the whole story is a good "tease," as we say in TV, for this little book about your rights as an American kid.

Mrs. Dixon told the sheriff what she heard about the purse . . . He found it, along with other evidence about the crime. Oliver was arrested, convicted in a jury trial, and sentenced to two years in jail.

Justice at work?

Not according to the American Civil Liberties Union, which sent lawyers in, mouths blazing, to argue to the court that Lacy's constitutional rights had been violated when her mother eavesdropped on her "private" conversation with her beloved mugger. So what? Well, that meant what Mrs. Dixon heard had not been legally obtained and therefore could not be used as evidence in a trial.

Does that argument make any sense to you? Well, it did to the state's supreme court. The judges agreed that the girl's right to privacy had been violated, so Oliver's conviction was thrown out of court. (He was convicted in a second trial without Mrs. Dixon's testimony, but that's another story.)

Now, it's cool that we all have a right to privacy and that we are free to see to it that it's enforced, but there are a couple of things to think about here. First, does a parent *not* have the right to protect a child from harm? And in this case, wasn't Mrs. Dixon trying to do just that by overseeing her daughter's ties with an obvious criminal? You have your opinion, and others will have other opinions.

Second, is a kid's personal privacy such a basic right that it cannot be overruled by the parent's right? And what about the mugging victim's rights in all of this? Again, you have your opinion, and others will have other opinions.

But with so many different opinions, how can we ever make sense out of situations like this? And how can we know which rights are more important than other rights?

Well, that's exactly what we're going to find out in this book. By the time you've finished reading the final chapter, I hope you'll understand the story of your own personal rights. It looks complicated, at first. But we're going to have some fun with all of this stuff, I promise you.

FIRST UP

You see it all the time on TV.

On cop shows, on news programs like mine, someone is yelling, "Hey, I know my rights!"

Well, maybe that person does, but probably not.

Sometimes it's just a lot of stupid shouting. Showing off. Like the Spartans and Persians in the movie *300*. They give a bad name to "discussion of rights."

But, hey, your rights are very important to your life. In this country, the reason they exist at all is because smart, brave, honorable people fought—and still fight!—to make them work for you and for every other American.

Especially you, kid.

Listen up: Even though you're not an adult yet, you're just as much an American as anyone is. That includes your parents, your teachers, your boss, and the cop on the block.

BUT . . . do you have the same rights as they do?

No, you don't.

So, what's the difference?

Well, there are many, many differences. Sometimes the differences exist for good reasons . . . sometimes those reasons are debatable.

That's what this book is all about. When we finish this trip together, I hope you'll feel that you know more than most people your age (and maybe some adults, too) about what your rights as a kid actually are. (And are not.)

So, do any of these "rights" we've been talking about have anything to do with issues you really care about, like whether or not your school can keep you from wearing clothes that show off your bare midriff? Or whether your school locker can be searched by school officials without your permission? Or whether you can bring your date to the senior prom, even if she is enrolled at another school?

You bet they do. That is exactly what we're talking about. All of these are cases where you think you ought to be able to do something that other people—parents, school, community—say that you definitely cannot do.

Let's face it. Many American kids are complete morons. So are many American adults. As I say on TV, the Constitution gives all Americans the right to be a moron, and a lot of us exercise that right every day.

When I use the word *moron*, I am referring to people who are simply too lazy to figure out what their country is all about.

Can your school keep you from wearing clothes that show off your bare midriff?
© Thinkstock/Corbis

Yeah, they like the freedom to have fun and have stuff, but they don't want to learn about how that freedom came to them.

You, kid, are an American. You have an obligation to be a good citizen. That means that you should be honest and pay attention to what happens in the United States and in the rest of the world, too. The iPods, computers, cell phones, and Black-Berries are fine, but you need to get out of yourself once in a while and look around in order to see and understand what is actually happening here in your America.

Many kids simply do not do that. Don't be one of them.

!PRODUCT WARNING!

In this book, I'm not going to talk about your rights under criminal law. For example, I'm not going to discuss whether or not you will be tried as an adult or juvenile if you are accused of committing certain crimes. I hope you don't NEED to know any of that stuff. If you DO, you need a lawyer. What I want us to talk about are your rights as a law-abiding, hardworking, fun-loving individual kid. In other words, we're talking about your rights to a fair shake in life, when you give life a fair shake back.

Knowing your rights and respecting them will make you a better person and a more successful one. Just by reading this book you are demonstrating that you are way ahead of the pack.

It's doubtful that Britney Spears would have read this book when she was your age. And look what's happened to her. The woman keeps forgetting her undergarments! I guess she has a right to do that but, I mean, come on!

I also want you to know a little bit about where your rights come from and (get this!) how, sometimes, you might be able to change things, when you feel that events controlled by someone else are unfair. Yes, that's possible. It's been done.

But don't be a wiseguy or wisegal. Standing up for your rights does not mean you should complain about every little thing that bugs you. Smarten up and appreciate the fact that you have opportunities kids in most other countries don't have. In China, if you mouth off to your teacher or parents, you could find yourself in a work camp. In the Muslim world, a bare midriff on a girl could get her a severe beating in front of the entire town. In Africa, millions of kids have little food to eat. Think about that the next time you pull up to McDonald's or Pizza Hut.

So I want you to know your rights, but I also want you to appreciate them and use them for everybody's well-being, not just your own. That's my plan here.

The truth will let you know how free you are, but it will not allow you to avoid your responsibility. That's correct: Kids have a responsibility to their country, parents, and brothers and sisters, as I've mentioned.

So, let's understand each other. We're going to be talking

about your rights according to the law. If you know how to con your parents, your teachers, or anyone else into letting you have your way all the time, that's something else. I don't want to hear about it. Shame on you, shame on them. This is not a book for selfish, spoiled brats. This is a book for kids who want to do what is right. Kids who want to be good Americans! I hope that's you!

KIDS ARE AMERICANS TOO

1

HOW CAN YOU BE A GOOD AMERICAN?

eing a good American starts with knowing your rights . . . and respecting the rights of others. And by doing the right thing when many other kids are not.

First off, your rights were not delivered by God to Moses on Mount Sinai.

That was the Ten Commandments, okay? (Hope you've heard of them.)

No, the rights you enjoy today were crafted by human hands and human minds. You have to get that straight from the start or you could go crazy. They were set down by a group of intelligent, difficult, argumentative, arrogant guys whom we officially call the "Founding Fathers." You've seen the marble busts and statues, the paintings of the very serious-looking old guys standing in great halls.

Don't be fooled by how they look.

Believe me, while they were Founding, the Fathers included brilliant thinkers, pains in the butt, more than one certifiable drunk, heroes who stood against the majority on principle, athletes (some of whom were skilled at chasing skirts), and speakers who could make the walls shake. In other words, this collection of true patriots (yes, I mean that term) was very, very human.

To repeat, you have to understand that.

See, your rights here in America were created by a wide range of people (except, owing to the times, they were all male and white). They differed because they had a diversity of human talents and human flaws. Not really so unlike the population of your school.

But what they shared was the most important thing. It can legitimately be called a "Vision." Let me sum it up in my words!

The average person in America should be free from unjust interference in daily life . . . and should be protected from the bad guys, whoever and wherever they are.

These Founding Fathers wanted to express this Vision in writing so it would live on even long after they were gone. The document they created is what we know as the U.S. Constitution.

Simple? Sounds like it.

But something like this had never happened before in the history of the world.

So, along with everything else, the Founding Fathers—screaming and swearing at each other, laughing and celebrating and pounding each other on the back—were Patriots with a capital *P*. More than 220 years ago, they were looking out for you.

They wanted to establish some ground rules that would be really easy for everyone to understand and really difficult for bad guys to mess up. They wanted to make the best possible country for Americans forever. That would include you and me . . . right now.

But, yes, they were human.

And they knew it.

Let's review: Well-meaning human beings created a set of rights and called it the Constitution. But they knew things would change over time. So what did they actually do for you?

Did they agree that you have the right to bring your iPod to gym class?

They did not.

Or maybe they did.Well, not specifically, but arguably.

That's right—we have the right to debate how the Constitution affects our lives today.

According to a recent news report, a thirteen-year-old girl in Minnesota told her parents, who are devout Roman Catholics, that she would not go to church with them ever again. "I know my rights," she said.

"You can't force me. The Constitution guarantees me freedom of religion, and I've decided to become a Wiccan!" Is she right about her rights?

No. She is not.

In cases like this, there has been general agreement in the legal community. Her parents have the right to make her go to church, if they choose. Her right to religious freedom is outweighed by her parents' right to raise her in their religion, until she leaves home.

Okay. This story has a kind of moral: As we talk more about rights, keep in mind that they are rarely absolute.

I mean, rights don't belong just to you. Your rights and my rights have to be balanced against the legitimate rights of other people as well.

That's easier said than done, I know. But here's a case where a young man did just that . . . He came up with a way to balance his right, as he saw it, with the rights of his school administrators.

YOUR HERO?

Do you have the right to refuse to do your school homework?

No.

Does the school have the right to assign so much of it that your life is ruined?

No. But I know it seems that way a lot of the time, no matter where you go to school.

Well, a fifteen-year-old kid thought hard about those questions, and then he took action. No, he didn't call the ACLU. He used his head. Read on—maybe Sean Gordon-Loeb will end up being one of your heroes.

As reported in the *New York Times*, Sean is one of the bright students at Stuyvesant High School, perhaps the most competitive high school in New York City. As in most communities today, the kids there often feel that they have too much homework. (When kids e-mailed me in response to my book *The O'Reilly Factor for Kids*, that was the Number One problem they wanted to talk about.) Some parents agree; others do not. Even the experts aren't sure where to draw the line.

But Sean, who by the way has an A-minus average, thought he knew. Vacations should be "downtime," he politely argued to the school's principal. What Sean wanted was elimination of all homework assignments during vacation, but the school prides itself on getting kids ready to compete for the country's best colleges.

The result? Compromise. The principal agreed to encourage teachers to lighten the homework assignments for vacation periods. One teacher had a very creative response, assigning a paper for vacation but allowing it to be turned in beforehand.

So, Sean's sensible approach to a problem—without *confrontation*—led to a balanced compromise. Remember Sean as we go forward. When you think you have the right to something—in this case, a worry-free vacation for relaxing—the first step should not be screaming your head off. Think. Be rational. Discuss the issue with respect.

Perhaps, like Sean, you, too, will be able to enjoy "the pursuit of happiness," a phrase we'll talk more about a little later. Go, Sean!

No pinhead, he!

A BLAST
FROM THE PAST

et's go back a bit . . .

These Founding Father guys got together in Philadelphia in 1787 . . .

Wait, wait! Don't let your eyes glaze over. It's a fascinating story—it really is! —and I hope you read all about it someday, if you haven't already. (Yes, I know from letters and e-mails to the *Factor* that some of you are just amazingly knowledgeable about history and politics, and I don't forget that.)

But I'm not going to tell that story in these pages.

What I want you to think about—and it's SAD

how many adults forget this basic fact—is that your rights were written down more than two *centuries* ago.

Not only were there no iPods then, there were no . . . Well, you name it: Look around your room, or your house, or the shopping mall. Ben Franklin, Thomas Jefferson, and the rest of the guys would be stunned if you somehow zipped them through time to our world today.

And it's not just the gadgets, look at the people. Every census shows remarkable changes in age, national heritage, language, and so forth among the Americans around you.

This is not 1787. Back then Americans ate parsnips. Had any of those lately? Ben Franklin and Thomas Jefferson would not believe what we are eating today! Have a taco, boys. How about some sushi? Pizza with mozzarella?

The point is, times have really changed in just about every way. Except, that is, for our rights. But even those are subject to new rulings based upon the modern age. And that fact can make your life confusing. New technology means kids have more access to "stuff" than any other kids in history.

But the most important difference for you and your rights is that IDEAS have changed since 1787.

You know some of the obvious ones. Back then, the creators of the Constitution—again, the basis for all American rights, the supreme law of the land—did not set down for women a right to vote. They also did not set down guarantees for full citizenship for African-Americans. They even allowed slavery. Not good. And

**KIDS ARE
AMERICANS TOO**

the entire country paid the price later in the bloody Civil War.

INTERLUDE OF RANTING: Hey, why should I respect the U.S. Constitution if it disrespects me? Huh? Am I included if I'm a woman? No way. Or if I'm African-American? No, no, no! Or if I'm not a property owner? What can that old rag mean to me in my life today?

Okay, so that's the puzzle right there.
How does this old set of rules keep working?
And does it really?
If you watch my TV program or listen to my radio program, you know that people are arguing about that question all over the country.
So let's join in . . .

UNINTENDED CONSEQUENCES

Has your American-history teacher ever told you that dinosaurs were given a berth on Noah's Ark during the Great Flood described in the Old Testament? Did he or she ever tell you that you belong in hell if you don't believe in the message of Jesus?

You are amazed by my questions. "Has O'Reilly lost his mind at last?" you ask (to yourself, I hope).

Well, in a high school in New Jersey, an American-history

teacher said these things and many more that, you would think, have nothing to do with the official class subject. Moreover, you could say that these statements are pretty good evidence of religious fanaticism.

How do we know for sure that the teacher said these things? Because sixteen-year-old Matthew LaClair taped these remarks in class (thereby becoming a part of American history himself). He thought it was his right to be taught American history, not fundamentalist Christian ideas.

Can you guess what happened next? I couldn't have. The teacher was replaced by another but assigned to teach the same subject to a new group of students. The school board banned taping in all classes without prior permission from the teacher. Some of Matthew's classmates got angry that the tapes appeared on the Internet and on TV, in effect airing their voices without their permission. Matthew alleges that the school did not step in to keep other kids from harassing him. He received a death threat.

There's more, but that's enough. Matthew's family is now suing the local board of education, and the beat goes on.

Is this a case of one courageous kid standing up for his rights to free speech? The "free speech" in this case, of course, is going public about the teacher's comments. Is this (also?) a case of one boy defending freedom of religion, meaning that he doesn't have to listen in school to material that is associated with Christian fundamentalism?

Maybe it started out that way, but now it's one heck of a mess.

New rules, lawyers on both sides, angry quotes in the press, kids choosing up sides. To me, the lesson is pretty clear. The teacher was way over the line, but Matthew's unusual action stoked the fire. His classmates may be acting badly, but they felt they were dragged into something they didn't want to become involved in. School officials may talk the talk about keeping religion out of the classroom, but they are steaming because the whole thing got so much public attention. (And this book is another example of that!)

As I've said before, sometimes it's better all around—better for your friends and your school and your community—if you try tact first. Matthew said the recordings were necessary because, otherwise, officials would not believe him. Maybe he's right. We'll never know. Maybe the officials would have covered the behind of the teacher, a fourteen-year-veteran. Again, we'll never know.

What we do know is that a lot of people are angry, and it looks as if neither side, so far, is happy with the outcome. Matthew's a kid like you, and he'll learn a lot from this. I hope he learns only good things. And I hope you learn that conflict like this should be thoughtfully, skillfully avoided.

In my opinion, Matt should have kept his tapes private, using them as notes. He should have stated his objections clearly and calmly to school administrators, and if they did not believe him, then he should have let them hear the taped remarks in private.

Going public with the tapes should have been the very last resort. If Matthew had taken the steps I suggest, I believe he would have won an early victory.

Months later, there was a final (one hopes) foot-note to all of this.

In a settlement between the LaClair family and the town board of education—one of those agreements, by the way, in which no one admits any "wrongdoing" in the matter under debate—Matthew won two points.

The board decided to ask the state's chapter of the Anti-Defamation League to begin teaching both students and their teachers about the need for public schools to keep ideas of church and state separate.

Also, the board offered to praise publicly Matthew's "courage and integrity" while the kid's parents in turn agreed to applaud that body for its actions.

After all of this was over, the boy himself felt that he had learned "how hard it can be sometimes to go against the grain, and that a lot of times, even though things may be tough, you still have to go through with it and finish it."

Sounds good. I'm okay with that. But I still recommend cool heads over hot words, whenever that's possible. When two sides have to agree to commend each other in public, that's ridiculous.

3

WHAT IS YOUR FREEDOM ALL ABOUT?

For openers, the Constitution guarantees all of us, in a famous phrase, "life, liberty and the pursuit of happiness."

Fair enough. Who could argue with that? I want to live, and I bet you do, too. I want to be free; so do you. We both want to "pursue happiness" . . .

Uh-oh. Just what the heck does that mean? Well, let's say we're both taking a train (after all, I do live in the New York City area): Is it okay for you to "pursue happiness" by shouting into your cell phone while I'm trying to read? Your happiness, in that case, causes me unhappiness. And the reverse. My happiness—seeing to it that you shut the heck up—would cause you unhappiness.

To put it simply, a great deal of the Constitution and everything based upon it in American law is an attempt—constantly changing and constantly challenged—to figure out how we can both be happy.

And there are only two of us in that scenario! What about the other three hundred million Americans?

The key to resolving our differences on the train involves asking this question: What policy is best for the majority of the people riding the railroad? Is it allowing everybody to shout? Of course not. That would create chaos.

So the train company has the right to make rules that override your right to shout into your phone. The train company has an obligation to think about the "greater good" of its passengers and to provide public satisfaction and safety. The train company is in business to make a profit, and your screaming will not further that cause.

Get it? Your right to free and loud speech is trumped by the train company's rights because you chose to get on the train. Once you make that choice, you sacrifice some personal freedom. If you don't like it, start your own train company. Call it the Screaming Eagle.

As you read, America is adding thousands of new citizens every day. Does each one of us get our own set of rights to make certain that we're always happy?

Of course not.

Then how does it work?

Let's look at the quick answer.

The Constitution does not exactly list all of your rights. Instead, it sets up the process for doing that and serves as a general reminder in all situations that your rights leave off at the spot where mine begin, and vice versa. But what does that mean?

I'm going to explain in one pithy paragraph something definitely worth knowing . . . something that many too many adults don't understand, and something that is really very simple!

> The Constitution sets down basic guidelines,
> but it also opens the door for additions in
> response to specific changes in our country.
> Remember, every time a new invention
> appears in stores, it brings with it new questions
> about "rights." Seven-hundred-watt car stereo
> amps did not exist in 1789. And loud music played
> by you can violate the rights of someone else.
> Right? I mean, who wants to hear 50 Cent at
> midnight being blared throughout the neighborhood
> streets? Give us a break, please.

Back in 1789, the Philadelphia gang themselves added ten ideas, or amendments, that we know as the Bill of Rights. (How many adults know the phrase, but don't really know what it means? Plenty, let me tell you from my experiences on the air.)

The truth is, most of your rights as a kid today are based upon those first ten amendments. That's the first thing to know here.

Second, the Philadelphia guys made it possible for the states to add (or deny) new changes, or amendments, to the original ten. Among other things, these amendments have given women the right to vote and have established full citizenship for members of racial minorities.

That's why, 220 years later, we're still coming up with new ideas about rights, still arguing with one another. Like, should there be an amendment guaranteeing equal rights between men and women in *all* things? Like, should there be an amendment denying gays the right to marry? (That would be the proposed Federal Marriage Amendment.)

See, an amendment to the Constitution is a valuable, powerful instrument in national law. It should not be treated as just another ornament on the Christmas tree, especially when new laws passed by Congress or the state houses can address and remedy (we can hope) an issue more speedily and efficiently than yet another constitutional amendment. (Right now, for the record, there are twenty-seven of them.)

So, summing up: You have rights, but so do other Americans. When your rights clash with theirs, a decision has to be made as to who wins.

Sometimes parents, teachers, or police make the decisions; sometimes the whole mess has to go to court. That's why lawyers make money.

Anyway, read on . . . The more you know about "rights," the better off your life will be. In every way.

Handy Rights Check

Before you wage a big battle over what you think is a denial of your rights, ask yourself the following questions:

Does getting my right . . .

Get in someone else's way?	[ ] Yes	[ ] No
Cause me more trouble than it's worth?	[ ] Yes	[ ] No
Require a long, drawn-out lawsuit?	[ ] Yes	[ ] No
Matter, really, all that much?	[ ] Yes	[ ] No

There's a simple but wise phrase I like a lot: "Don't sweat the small stuff." This rights business is for the big stuff. Let go of minor annoyances, like the things you squabble with your brother or sister about and instead fight over the issues that really matter to you.

ASK
O'REILLY!
(A Special Feature)

You: How old do I have to be to use a gun when I go hunting with my father?

O'Reilly: I dunno.

You: You, uh, dunno?

O'Reilly: No, I don't.

You: (after a pause) But you just got me to read this book about my rights. Isn't that a right?

O'Reilly: Could be. Probably is.

You: (mumbling) What a crock . . .

O'Reilly: Could you speak up?

You: What a crock!

O'Reilly: Not at all.

You: But, but—

O'Reilly: Okay, we're at a really important place here. Follow me closely. Number one, there are a gazillion different kinds of rights and nonrights because there are a gazillion different laws. (Well, maybe not quite that many.)

You: Then how can I learn them all?

O'Reilly: You can't. What you learn is, how to find out what they are, and how they work. But there's something else . . . Number two, those Founding Father guys in Philadelphia were very suspicious of a big government (like today's government in Washington). They believed that a lot of laws—a lot of rights— should be decided by the individual state, or even the individual county or city.

You: But I want to go hunting with my father, and I'm only eleven years old.

O'Reilly: Then you better live in a state where the state's lawmakers have decided that you and your dad have that right. There are fifty states, and each one makes its own laws on many issues that affect you. I'm sure you know from kid gossip that driver's licenses and drinking laws are handled differently in different states. No book is going to list all of those laws; the length of that list would be about the equivalent of a hundred *Harry Potters*. Besides, you don't need to know the hunting laws in Hawaii if you want to go deer hunting in upstate New York.

You: So that's why you "dunno."

O'Reilly: You got it. As I said, this is very important to understand. Some laws, like kidnapping laws, are the same for every state; they're determined by the U.S. Congress in Washington. Many, many more are decided by the lawmakers in state capitals, county courthouses, and city halls.

You: What a mess.

O'Reilly: Can be. But once you understand that point, you're on your way to understanding where rights come from and just how they work.

I hope you enjoyed the special feature above; there will be more as we go along.

Oh, and one more thing: To know your rights, you have to ask the "right" questions. In your school library there should be books about what the laws are in your state. Want to go hunting? Look up the law. (You can do this on the Internet as well.) Be proactive! That means, be curious and find out what you are legally entitled to do.

One good source is *Teen Rights: A Legal Guide for Teens and the Adults in Their Lives,* by attorney Traci Truly. In an appendix she lists several basic laws for each of the fifty states, such as the right to have an abortion, minimum age for marriage, and child labor restrictions. I think you'll be surprised at the differences between the states in regard to such issues.

Anyway, if you research the basic laws affecting young people in your state, you'll be the smartest kid around!

And despite what some pinheads might say, smart kids are usually admired and respected.

Not a bad thing, kid.

FIFTY STATES...

EACH ONE RATES...

FIFTY DIFFERENT LAWS...
THAT'S JUST BECAUSE...

EACH STATE
SETS ITS TONE...

HAS ITS OWN (LAWS)...

SO WHAT'S UP
WHERE YA LIVE?...

I MEAN, READ ON!
ON AND ON AND ON...

READ ON!

(wild applause)

Hey, you'd rather hear Ludacris?
I hope not.

REALITY CHECK

Let's say that Rufus Blowhard, presidential candidate, loudly proclaims that he's against the death penalty. Hates it. Won't ever vote for it. If you agree, should you support him? Let's also say his opponent, Serena Mellow, fiercely and loudly disagrees with him in every speech, arguing instead that the death penalty should not be abolished, but rather should be extended to cover even more crimes. If you agree, should you vote for her? Before you cast your ballot, consider this:

National law almost never applies to a death sentence. The states make these decisions. Maybe Rufus wants you to think he has a soft side. Maybe Serena wants you to think she's really tough. Fine in both cases. But some of the most ridiculous people I deal with these days don't understand this basic fact: The president may be the most powerful man or woman on the planet, but our guys in Philadelphia put limits on the job description. (Again, people won't agree about the exact nature of those limits, keeping lawyers and judges and spin masters busy.) But just know that our Founding Fathers wanted a president, not a king. Because a king could take away your rights, couldn't he? . . . And he did in 1775. That's why the patriots in America told King George to take a hike, and beat his red-coated army.

No one should be allowed to take away another person's rights! No one.

AWESOME

multiple-choice quiz no. 1

Okay, time to see how much we learned . . .
Select just one answer for each question. No cheating!

1. Your rights in America are . . .
   a. Just like those of a kid your age in China.
   b. Earned by extra homework assignments.
   c. Unique in the world because of the Constitution.
   d. The result of Angelina Jolie's hard work for you.

2. I'm trying in this book to convince you to . . .
   a. Tell your parents to take a hike.
   b. Learn what your rights are—and are not.
   c. Memorize the Bill of Rights.
   d. Write a letter to your congressman.

3. The "Founding Fathers" are known for . . .
   a. Crafting the U.S. Constitution.
   b. Setting up orphanages after the Civil War.
   c. Banning alcohol at the Constitutional Convention.
   d. Introducing gangsta rap to Massachusetts.

4. Every teen in America has the right to . . .

   a. Get free broadcasts of all pro baseball games.

   b. Get a driver's license at age sixteen.

   c. Play on the varsity team of his/her favorite sport.

   d Have a home life free from abuse.

5. Your attendance at church, synagogue, or mosque . . .

   a. Depends upon your feelings in the morning.

   b. Is the choice of your parents.

   c. Should be approved by your guidance counselor.

   d. Is considered a sign of good citizenship.

How'd you do?

Here are the answers:

1. c; 2. b; 3. a; 4. d; 5. b.

Stay alert. I have several more of these multiple-choice opportunities up ahead. What do you win if you answer correctly?

My respect!

4 LAST PIECE OF THE RIGHTS PUZZLE: LISTEN UP!

Quick Review:

1. Your rights started with a document written by human beings.
2. Those smart guys made it flexible by setting up a system for changes (amendments).
3. They also erected a strong fence/barrier/moat between the national government (that would be Washington) and state governments (legislators where you live).

But if the president, along with other representatives of the national (federal) government, is restricted by the Constitution in certain ways—meaning that he or she does NOT have unlimited powers—can the lawmakers in your state do whatever they want to do? The answer is no.

If the Constitution (in your view) can be interpreted to mean that you, an ambitious girl who likes playing football, have the right to play on your school's all-boys football team when there's no girls' team, what happens when your state or local government, or your local school board, disagrees?

This, my young friend, is where the real fun begins.

And also where the craziness, the anger, and the whole gamut of other human emotions come in . . .

See, there is a third party involved in defining your rights in this great land: the court system.

If you watch my program, you know that I frequently rant and rail against court decisions that—IN MY VIEW—are ridiculous, dangerous, or just plain wrong. (Don't get me started!)

But I respect the SYSTEM—at least, the intent behind the system, as the Philadelphia gang saw it. See, there has to be a referee, an umpire, when your state lawmakers pass a law that other free citizens believe is unfair. The buzzword, as you certainly know if you have been following public life in this country, is *unconstitutional*.

Let's go back to that train we talked about earlier . . .

You're on your cell phone shouting louder and louder because

Can your school board keep girls from playing sports on an all-boys team?
© AP/Ron Schwane

we've entered a tunnel, or your friend's signal is breaking up: "Hello! HELLO! I CAN'T HEAR YOU!!"

Meanwhile, I am trying to read and concentrate on, say, the latest edition of *The Collected Thoughts of Paris Hilton*. (A very heavy book.)

Does the law help us here? Well, it might, and it might not. Suppose it's vague, something to the effect that passengers should respect one another's rights. That's not going to help us very much.

So, one of us, annoyed with the other, might get a lawyer to go to the courts for an interpretation of the law. And our argument will be that it has to be interpreted by the ideas of the men who wrote the Constitution—that's what's called "original intent."

If our local court in New York disagrees with me, I can take the case up to the top court in the state. And if THAT court disagrees with me (and I still have enough money left for the lawyer), I can take it all the way to Washington to the Supreme Court.

There, one of two things is likely to happen.

They can refuse to hear my case because they don't think the Constitution applies directly to it or because they have better things to do or for no reason at all. (The nine judges—the Supremes, as some people like to call them—don't have to explain why they won't hear a case.)

Or, they can decide to hear it. By a simple majority of only 5–4, say, they can interpret the law so that it applies to every one of us, no matter where we live. And we have to obey the law, or we could be punished.

That is the real power in the USA.

O'REILLY SWINGS

Okay, this will help you remember how the Supreme Court works . . .

Let's say that four of the judges always agree on one side of an issue, and four others always agree on the opposite side—no matter what the issue is. This doesn't take much imagination, because it has happened a lot.

Now this takes some imagination: I have been appointed as the ninth judge!

Think about it . . . Bill O'Reilly, your humble TV journalist, is now the so-called swing vote on the Supreme Court of the United States.

No, no, don't wake up screaming yet.

Think about it.

You probably wouldn't be reading this little book if you didn't know something about me, my program, and my opinions.

Your worst nightmare!
Judicial robes © Glyn Jones/Corbis.
Photograph of Bill O'Reilly courtesy
of Lynn McCann.

Death penalty?* I'm against it, for many reasons. Equal opportunity in jobs and education? I'm for it.

So when a case comes before the court, my vote is the only one that counts, and you can pretty much guess how I'm going to vote. Again, imagine me in my black robes as the swing vote on the Supreme Court and you can see how important these guys and gals can be. In fact, a lot of experts believe that the most important act of any president is his or her choice of judges to nominate for the highest court in the land.

Okay, you can wake up now . . .

★ ★ ★

And that is why people on all sides work so hard to make sure that the judges selected and approved are at all levels smart, honorable, and fair—if that's possible. These men and women can have the last say about your rights in a million situations.

---

* The death penalty is too easy for Osama bin Laden and others like him. They deserve to suffer every day in a hard-labor situation. In my opinion, that would be a greater deterrent than a quick execution. Also, some innocent people have been executed. Not good.

This just in from our Sad News for Teens Reporter. Listen up, kids . . . The trend in American court decisions is to favor the rights of schools to prevent you from doing just about anything that they regard as distracting from the educational process. Does sexy clothing distract other students from their math homework? (Well, duh.) Does a political statement on a T-shirt distract someone who disagrees with you? This is the kind of thing that causes many controversies. Bottom line from the Sad News Staff: Usually, you kids don't win.

ARE THE SUPREMES YOUR FRIENDS?

Having trouble sleeping lately?

Then try reading some court decisions, especially those of the Supreme Court. I mean, how do they keep themselves awake while writing these things?

Okay, they're not writing for you and me; they're trying to

define a right very, very clearly, and they're trying to justify a decision by interpreting specific parts of the Constitution. And that's only the beginning.

Your eyes are glazing over already . . .

So I'm not going to go into the details of a decision on paddling, say, that could run on for twenty pages.

But here are a couple of examples that will help you understand how tricky things can get.

Way back in 1975 (I know, I know, you weren't even born yet), the Supremes agreed to listen to a lawsuit brought by nine Colorado kids who felt that they had been expelled from school without being given a hearing. (The technical way to say this is that they were denied due process under the Fourteenth Amendment to the Constitution.)

In brief, the majority of the judges decided that schools should be required, usually, to discuss a student's proposed suspension quickly and listen to his or her side of the story before taking action.

So, by a vote of 5 to 4(!), the Supremes did a solid for you: Kids had to be given a hearing before they were kicked out. And in hearings, sometimes minds can be changed.

Two years later, two Florida boys filed a lawsuit against school officials to argue that being paddled on the butt was against the Eighth Amendment—in other words, it was "cruel and unusual punishment."

They also argued that they should have had a hearing to explain their side of the story before being paddled. Again, their lawyers were talking about "due process" in the Fourteenth Amendment.

(Are you on to my wicked plan yet? I'm trying to convince you that these dull old phrases in eighteenth-century English are right up-to-the-minute in your daily school lives.)

As it happens, Florida school officials had been very precise in their use of paddling. For example, according to a regulation, the instrument involved should be "a flat wooden paddle measuring less than 2 feet long, 3 to 4 inches wide, and about 1/2 inch thick." These people meant business. (And I believe I have your attention here.)

The majority of the judges decided that (1) they weren't going to agree that paddling is necessarily "cruel and unusual" and (2) they weren't going to insist that officials have a hearing before paddling because that would be "a significant intrusion" into the educational process.

Yep, the decision was 5 to 4. This time, the Supremes, you might think, were not on your side. In some schools, kids who misbehave *can* be paddled! Usually, the local school board decides. You'll never get paddled in liberal San Francisco. But in conservative Mississippi, watch your butt, literally.

PORN JUDGMENT?

Here's another instance where you could ask whether or not the judges are on your side.

The Supreme Court Justices. Seated in the front row from left to right are Associate Justice Anthony M. Kennedy, Associate Justice John Paul Stevens, Chief Justice of the United States John G. Roberts, Associate Justice Antonin Scalia, and Associate Justice David Souter. Standing from left to right in the top row are Associate Justice Stephen Breyer, Associate Justice Clarence Thomas, Associate Justice Ruth Bader Ginsburg, and Associate Justice Samuel Alito Jr.

© AP/J. Scott Applewhite

In 1996, the Supremes nixed the Communications Decency Act, which was created by Congress to limit kids' access to pornography on the Internet.

Two years later, Congress tried again with the Child Online Protection Act. The idea was simple: Make it a crime for anyone to run a Web site that lets kids in to see "harmful" material.

"Harmful"? Well, Congress was trying. See, it's very difficult to define *pornography* in a way that most people will agree with. Bet even you and your friends can't! In fact, there's a famous line from a Supreme Court judge who said, "I can't define it, but I know it when I see it." Nice try, Your Honor.

But we pretty much know what Congress was attempting to do. Still, a federal judge knocked down the law as unconstitutional. His argument: "Perhaps we do the minors of this country harm if First Amendment protections, which they will with age inherit fully, are chipped away in the name of their protection."

In other words, he felt that, in trying to protect kids from porn on the Internet, this law interfered with the free-speech rights of adults. (That would be you, in a few years.) So, you can download porn now, if that's your thing, because otherwise adults wouldn't be able to.

So, what do you think of that logic? Even if you never ever want to download porn, not ever, you the kid now or you the adult in the future, what does this decision mean to you? Is it necessary? Does it leave children exposed to harm?

I don't want my children exposed to such filth, but I'm the type of parent who makes sure they don't go near it. The real concern here is for children who don't have parents with the will, the time, the means, or the smarts to monitor Internet activity. What about them?

I'm asking you to think about this and come to your own conclusion. This is not a book, as you've already discovered, with simple answers. This situation is what scientists call "a thought problem." Think it out. Talk it out. You might be surprised at how many different reactions you get to this story.

So, The Supremes: Friends or Not?

There's no easy answer. And each time, just that one vote made the difference in cases that greatly affected kids' lives. In Ohio, the suspensions were for ten days. You know what that can do to a kid's school year, on all levels. These are big deals. As for paddling, you have your reasons for avoiding the swats, and some of you have parents who agree with you. They might even argue that their parental rights include the right to protect you from physical punishment. But that's another, uh, court case.

So, again, let's review:

The smart guys in Philly set down a Vision in the Constitution for protecting Americans and for being fair . . . then they created a device for amending that Vision over time . . . they also gave the states and the national government separate powers to enact laws . . . and THEN they gave the courts the job of determining whether or not (in their judgment) each law is actually constitutional.

I've oversimplified the process (and you can thank me for that), but the above paragraph, basically, explains what you need to know in order to understand just what your rights are in this country.

This sixteen-year-old kid down somewhere in the Southeast has a license from his state to ride his motorcycle . . . which he bought with his own money after working hard at the local Wal-Mart for several months . . . and his parents have agreed to let him ride the thing during daylight hours if he always wears a helmet—BUT!!—his high school principal won't allow anyone to ride a motorized two-wheel vehicle to school and park it on school property. See, she believes that the stats on motorcycle accidents prove that the bike is about twice as dangerous for a kid to ride in traffic as a car. Is the principal correct? Does it matter? Does the kid have a right to ride his bike onto school property since he's clearly fufilled all legal requirements? Well, he could go to court, but he would likely lose. The principal determines what happens on school property. The kid has followed all the rules, except one: her rule. In this case, that's the one that counts more than any of the others.

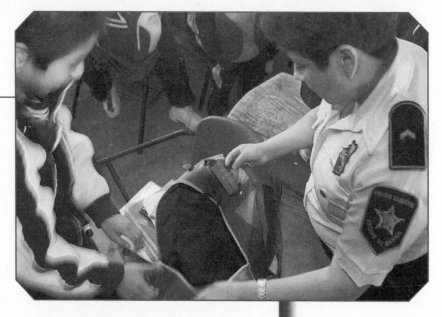

Do schools have the right to search your belongings without probable cause? You may be surprised by the answer.
© Keith Dannemiller/Corbis

In many ways this situation is a lot like the train situation we talked about earlier. You will recall that because the train is private property, the train company has the right to make rules such as "no loud noise" provided these rules are reasonable, intended for the good of the passengers, and do not discriminate against any one specific group.

Like it or not, noisy commuters need to pipe down or walk.

Similarly, school administrators, more often than not, have

the right to establish rules on closed campuses, provided they, too, are reasonable rules, serve the greater good of the student body, and do not discriminate against any one specific group, even if the school is a public institution.

Here's an example that upsets a lot of people: students, their parents, their lawyers.

It involves an important constitutional concept called "probable cause." Just as the phrase "I know my rights!" is often used and misused on cop shows, so, too is this phrase, although you probably have to listen closely to hear it. Usually, the stern judge or worried district attorney is questioning the cops about whether or not they had probable cause to take some action that uncovered vital evidence in a crime. If there was no probable cause, then the evidence gets tossed.

But here's the thing for you, kid. The definition of *probable cause* for a student on school property is much looser, much wider, than it is for adults in similar circumstances outside of school.

I'm serious! Your school officials can use a different concept to justify searching you, your car, or your locker for, say, weapons or illegal drugs than the police can use to search an adult they think possesses one of those things. The term that applies to you kids is *reasonable suspicion*.

Define, please.

Well, don't even try. You don't need that kind of headache at your time of life.

See, the definition of *reasonable suspicion* (and of *probable cause,* but that's another can of worms) is going to depend upon what your principal thinks, what your school board has decided, and what local courts have said in disputed cases.

You're not happy about this . . . Or are you?

On the one hand, if you are determined to bring a concealed ninja weapon to school, reasonable suspicion means that you are more likely to be searched—and have that evidence stand up in any legal proceeding—than an adult would be doing the same thing in a mall. If he or she conceals the weapon cleverly, there may be, in that situation, no probable cause to search him or her. Your school official, though, needs only to feel reasonable suspicion. So, maybe you think this is unfair.

On the other hand, if you're a student who does not want to be walking down the hall next to someone carrying a concealed ninja weapon (no matter how, uh, cool that is, right?), you might think that this "reasonable suspicion" thing is pretty fair. It gives more weight to your rights as a sane, decent kid than to the rights of the nut case with the throwing star.

We really should talk a lot more about the whole school thing and the rights you have there because, as you know, school is a major part of your life. Isn't it? So let's do that . . .

5 YOUR LIFE IN THE SCHOOL DAZE

Actually, your school, right now, IS your life.

I don't mean to knock family, part-time job, community service, church or synagogue or mosque—but in terms of hours spent in class, playing sports, doing homework, and (maybe) feeling hope or dread, school is pretty much your life.

You might know that I taught high school for a couple of years. What I remembered from my own difficult past in school was magnified several times as

I sat on the other side of the desk. In other words, God got revenge on me during my teaching days because I gave my own teachers such a hard time back when I was in high school!

Kid life can be hard. Kid life can be confusing. (But we're not focusing on those issues today. I've already written about them, in case you don't know, in *The O'Reilly Factor for Kids*.)

So (pardon the pun), how do we do the "rights" math in school?

Let's start with the truth: You want your own way, don't you?

Of course you do. And there's nothing wrong with that. We all want our own way. Well, most of us do. Sometimes a Mother Teresa comes along, someone who is completely generous. And thank God for people like that. But back to you . . .

You have a brain that knows the numbers just wouldn't work if you always get your own way. Why? Because then I wouldn't get my own way . . . and neither would your best friend or worst enemy . . . and neither would anyone else around you. And if that happened we would all GET TEED OFF!—and we'd probably take it out on you. Nobody could stand that pressure.

So we should forget our wants and focus on everybody's rights. That's how we draw the line, and learning to draw that line will make you very, very smart. And much happier as well.

Start being smart now . . . and you'll be even smarter when you legally become an adult (which will be sooner than you think).

I mean it! Making these distinctions will be essential to your "pursuit of happiness" for the rest of your life. Successful people who make lots of money and have great jobs are usually people who can convince others that they are fair! Not selfish, spoiled egomaniacs! So, the "right" deal will help you all throughout your life.

Meanwhile, there's something about the school situation that seems to inspire some pretty nutty debates about rights.

It gets crazier when religion is involved (see my previous book, *Culture Warrior*, for some goofy stories about Christmas and students' rights).

It also gets crazy when graduation is coming up. Maybe kids want to leave a lasting mark at school . . . or show that they're too cool for discipline. Whatever, graduation rituals, from prom nights to valedictory speechmaking, seem to inspire a lot of controversy.

WHEN IS A KNIGHT NOT A KNIGHT?

Last December, seventeen-year-old Patrick Agin's medieval costume caused a stir at his Rhode Island high school that ended up bringing in the state branch of the American Civil Liberties Union (ACLU). You may find this story pretty funny, or you may agree that it shows how complicated the rights business can be.

A senior at Portsmouth High School, Patrick has an interesting hobby: He acts out events from the Middle Ages with a group called the Society for Creative Anachronism. That means that these guys act out stuff that happened long ago as if it happened today.

And there's more. Patrick's mother sells reproductions of medieval armor—you know, the kind the knights wore. These reproductions are created by Patrick's uncle. Lively family, right?

Got the picture? Well, not to make another pun, but it is a picture that caused all the trouble. Patrick wanted to wear a knight's armor in his yearbook photo. Other kids have been allowed to use photos of themselves posed with their musical instruments or participating in sports, so it wasn't as if the school has a policy requiring suits and ties in yearbook photos.

But . . . it does have a policy that principal Robert Littlefield applied in Patrick's case. See, the kid not only wore his chain mail in the photo; he also carried a medieval sword.

Littlefield refused to allow the photo in the yearbook, explaining, "Students wielding weapons is just not consistent with our existing policies or the mission of the school." Translation: The school has in place a "zero-tolerance" weapons policy.

Do you think the principal was being unreasonable? Well, the ACLU argued that his action was "a perfect example of bureaucratic ridiculousness."

On his side, Littlefield noted that past graduating seniors had not been allowed to pose in their official senior photos with, for example, a musket used in reenactments of the U.S. Civil War. He had, however, allowed them to buy ads with such photos and made the same offer to Patrick.

What's wrong with this picture?
Photo by Leilani Eileen Martin Cardoza (Zaraphin)

The school and the ACLU agreed to take the matter to the Rhode Island commissioner of education. At first, the ACLU filed a lawsuit before a U.S. District Court judge, but he (in my view, wisely) suggested the matter be taken first to the Department of Education.

Which side won? Was there a compromise? What were the principles that applied?

Well, to sum up, the commissioner decided that the principal's decision had been "unreasonable and arbitrary."

He argued that "no tolerance for a yearbook photograph with a weapon becomes full tolerance when the family pays for the publication of the photograph." In other words, "tolerance for weapons can be purchased." This is illogical.

He also noted that in other sections of the yearbook students were shown with "a corn cob pipe, liquor bottles, a beer stein, toy guns, bows and arrows, swords, a knife, color guard rifle shapes, and an axe made of foil." (Is something going on out there I don't know about?)

What happened here, I think, is that everyone calmed down. Well, maybe not the ACLU lawyer (surprise!), who had to have the last word: "The Commissioner's ruling rightly rejects the knee-jerk use of zero tolerance policies by school officials that often run counter to both common sense and students' rights."

But I think the point is not to attack the principal, or anyone else, for having a point of view. The point is that Patrick's right to celebrate his love of medieval history in a certain way was reasonably discussed, examined, and upheld.

In another state, with another commissioner of education, the decision might have gone in a different direction. Personalities could have come into conflict. There might have been other factors to muddy the waters.

But Patrick's story is a good model for many situations, I think. By and large, it seems that people listened to each other. Reason and common sense won and so did Patrick. Score one for the kids!

Did I not tell you so on the cover of this book? *Kids Are Americans Too!*

AWESOME
multiple-choice quiz no. 2

1. Women have the right to vote because . . .
- a. Members of all racial minorities do, too.
- b. Thomas Jefferson wanted his wife to be able to vote for him.
- c. The Constitution has been amended.
- d. Our laws are based upon British laws.

2. The famous phrase "the pursuit of happiness" means that you . . .
- a. Can always download Hillary Duff for free.
- b. Are guaranteed a minimum wage.
- c. Can pursue your dream, but not prevent others from pursuing theirs.
- d. Are allowed to move across state lines.

3. Same-sex marriage . . .
- a. Is illegal now in every state in America.
- b. Costs the taxpayers $110 million each year.
- c. Was banned by the Founding Fathers.
- d. Would be banned by the proposed Federal Marriage Amendment.

4. Many laws that affect you are . . .

a. About as sane as Simon Cowell's comments on *American Idol.*

b. Made by your state, not the national government.

c. Only guidelines for behavior, not rules.

d. In effect only when you're outside the home.

5. If you are a girl, you can play on the boys football team if . . .

a. You are willing to sue the local school district.

b. Your parents belong to the PTA.

c. You explain the Bill of Rights to your teacher.

d. Your school administration okays it.

Here are the correct answers. I hope you can see why:

1. c; 2. c; 3. d; 4. b; 5. d.

How're you doing? Having fun yet?

ON THE OTHER HAND . . .

In another case related to graduation activities, eighteen-year-old Bilal Shareef brought a lawsuit against his school system in Newark, New Jersey, on religious grounds. Bilal, a practicing Muslim, graduated with a straight-A average from West Side High School in 2006. But since the ceremonies were held in a Christian church, he did not attend. He explained that he had been put in a "very, very uncomfortable" position.

Please take a moment to think about this, and then I'm going to tell you how the various sides weighed in (yes, there were more than two sides). If you're a practicing Roman Catholic, would you attend your high school graduation in a mosque? Listen up: I'm not taking sides here; I'm just asking you to form an opinion on your own, before we continue.

See, these things are much more fun if you decide what you think you believe, and then listen to others.

So here are the parties:

The ACLU (of course): Citing the state constitution, the ACLU argued that no one can be "compelled to attend any place of worship contrary to his faith and judgment." The compulsion, by their reasoning, came about because "the culmination of one's school career is at graduation."

The lawyer for the school district: He countered that "some use of religious facilities by public school districts" is allowed by state law. (For the record, the 2007 graduation was scheduled to be held in a secular concert hall.)

KIDS ARE
AMERICANS TOO

Bilal's father: Ahmad Shareef commented that he would have felt pride at seeing his son receive his diploma but was "even more proud that he stood up for our beliefs."

The executive director of the Islamic Society of North America: Although his organization represents some four hundred mosques, he remarked that he was not aware that any other Muslim high school student had objected to attending a school function in a church.

Now it's your turn. You've heard several different views. Was Bilal unreasonable? Should he have gone along with the majority of his school community? What other alternatives can you think of, ideas that might satisfy both sides? What did the school district intend by using the church?

Now that you've made your decision, do you want to know what the courts in New Jersey determined? Well, as of press time, the case was still being decided. Check out www.billoreilly .com for up-to-the-minute reports.

MUSICAL INTERLUDE

Rapster "Rights" O'Reilly, getting jiggy with Ben Franklin and Tom Jefferson!

DON'T GET MAD . . .

GET YOUR RIGHTS!

I MEAN, BEN TOLD ME . . .
I MEAN, TOM TOLD ME . . .

I'M TELLING YA NOW . . . YA GOTTA KNOW HOW

I MEAN, BEN TOLD ME . . .
I MEAN, TOM TOLD ME . . .

KNOWING WHAT IS TRUE WILL PROTECT YOU!

I MEAN, BEN TOLD ME . . .
I MEAN, TOM TOLD ME . . .

GET DOWN WITH THAT CREW—

UNDERSTAND WHAT IS TRUE!

No, I am not considering a career change, but you can see why music-industry agents are lining up outside my door, offering bling.

Remember, all of these lyrics are copyrighted.

(That's my right!)

This means you!

I'm not going into all of the gazillion messes that can occur when you download something, because you already know about the ones that affect your life.

But if you feel that you have the right to download a song for free because . . . well, because why, kid?

Okay, you want to argue that the music industry is a big monster that charges you too much, or something like that. I see your point. But what about that singer or band you like so much? They shouldn't make any money for their work? They should entertain you, and whomever you share the file with, for free? They don't have the right to get something for what they've created for you?

You know what I'm saying. And what about people who write books? (Ahem.) Or make movies? Music, words, pictures—these can all be used to invent fantasy worlds, but you really have the wrong fantasy about life if you don't realize that entertainment and information reach you because people work very, very hard. That's how I see it, anyway.

Whatever your opinion, this whole thing is going to be a very large part of your life. It's going to be one of the hottest debates about rights for your future in America. Just think about it in those terms, okay?

You: I want to wear a T-shirt at school that says SAVE THE MANATEES!

O'Reilly: That's a nice thought.

You: You bet it is! But my principal says it's a political slogan, and if he allows one, he has to allow all of the others.

O'Reilly: And some of those can get pretty rough . . .

You: So what? Don't I have the right to express myself in a decent way? Anyway, what would happen if I took the school to court and said the principal was denying my rights under the First Amendment?

O'Reilly: I dunno.

You: You dunno?

O'Reilly: (rolling eyes) Look, let's skip the next bit, okay? We'll cut to the chase . . . See, I don't know the judges who are sitting on the court in your state . . . Haven't heard anything about them, or what they think, or what decisions they've made in the past.

You: But this is a matter of law!

O'Reilly: (smiles sagely)

You: Well, isn't it?

O'Reilly: (smiles even more sagely)

You: Okay, I think I get it . . . Laws are made by human beings.

O'Reilly: And?

You: They're also interpreted by human beings.

O'Reilly: And so . . . ?

You: Well, even though I think it's clearly freedom of speech for me to wear a T-shirt that expresses my view, my right under the Constitution . . .

Does this pass the dress code?

O'Reilly: Even so, some judges might agree with you. Others might not.

You: This could make me dizzy.

O'Reilly: Watch my program. You'll meet quite a few people—on all sides of the issues—who are confused by this stuff. I mean, they're nuts! But you can figure it out. I have faith.

You: Really?

O'Reilly: Really. You just have to keep your head,

learn the rules and how they work, seek sane advice, and try to make sense of the arguments on the other side. Why is your principal so stubborn about the T-shirt? Understand his side—

You: But I want to wear the—

O'Reilly: Hey! I didn't say "agree" with his point of view. Understand where he's coming from. Then maybe you can make your view understandable to him. Maybe you can even persuade him.

You: You think I could win that argument?

O'Reilly: I dunno.

You: Okay, okay, I get it.

O'Reilly: See?

HIGH IDEALS?

But it's never that simple.

Did you hear the story about the kid who thought it was his right of free speech to put up a fourteen-foot-long banner reading BONG HITS 4 JESUS? I'm not making this up. (Uh, if you're exceptionally innocent, maybe I should explain that the phrase has to do

A question 4 the Supremes?
© Clay Good/ZUMA Press

with using marijuana. By the way, being innocent about drugs is not a bad thing. But knowing the score may protect you better.)

Back to our story . . .

Joseph Frederick, an eighteen-year-old senior at Juneau-Douglas High School in Alaska, displayed the banner as students of the school assembled outside to watch runners in the 2002 Olympics torch relay as they raced down the road. The principal, Deborah Morse, had the banner taken down and immediately suspended the kid for ten days.

As we will see again and again, things are not always exactly clear-cut.

See, the kid argued that he was not on school property, since everyone had gathered in the street outside. The principal shot back that the event was sponsored by the school, even though it took place on the sidewalk, so she had the right to get rid of the sign and punish him. The kid argued that he had the right to express his opinion about cannabis (yes, he was for it). Ms. Morse countered that his message undermined the school's educational mission and flew in the face of its antidrug stance. (True enough.) That, in her view, meant that she could keep Frederick from making his statement.

You noticed that I said "2002," right? But this case isn't over yet. When Frederick sued, a local court agreed with the school. Then a federal appeals court agreed with Frederick, saying that the school could not "punish and censor nondisruptive speech."

There's more. Now the Supremes have agreed to take the case. (By the way, the lawyer representing the school is Ken Starr, whom some of you may remember—I know, I know, just barely—from the Monica Lewinsky affair.)

This case is not just a matter of pride, by the way. If the school loses in the end, damages will have to be paid to Frederick.

What will happen? I don't know, although I'd guess that the current lineup of judges will side with the school. Whatever happens, you can be sure that I'll be talking about it on *The Factor.*

As for Frederick, he has said that he put up the banner so that it would be seen on TV. He sure got his wish. But judging by his slogan, Fred is a pinhead. Jesus and pot have nothing in common. This is just a case of a wiseguy making trouble.

But the Supreme Court is hearing it! That means, taking it seriously!

Yes, this really is a flash. Just as this book was sent off to the printer this past summer, the Supremes suddenly came down from the heights and spoke their several minds.

You're going to love this, especially after everything we've talked about. Better yet, you're going to understand it, precisely because of everything we have talked about. It's a great, right-here-and-now example of how complicated—and fascinating—the continuing story of rights in America can be.

If we could just cut to the chase, the box score would be Principal Morse 5, Joseph Frederick 4 (or 5 1/2 to 3 1/2, as you will see). Bottom line: Joseph's "prank" was not free speech protected by the First Amendment, according to the majority of the Supremes, and Ms. Morse does not have to pay damages to the kid because, to use the legal language, as a government official she is entitled to "qualified immunity" from liability.

So has everything about this case been cleared up now? Is everyone all across the land dancing happily through the streets, hand in hand, blowing bubbles to the same tune on our iPods?

You know better. Or you've been dozing off while reading this book.

As it turns out, this case took some crazy twists and turns, even after all we've already discussed and thought about. Get this: The ACLU—fervent advocates of perfectly free speech—was actually joined in their concern over this case by conservative religious groups like the American Center for Law and Justice (that would be a Pat Robertson entity).

What? Did Jesus really do bong hits back in the old days, pastor?

No. But think a little about this. The left believes that you have the right to state in school (or to argue in the school newspaper) that marijuana is a good thing. The right does not believe that (typically). But some conservatives were afraid that if Joseph Frederick wasn't permitted to preach in favor of getting stoned, a fundamentalist Christian kid couldn't speak out against abortion, premarital sex, evolutionary thought, or gay marriage, either.

So some people on the right supported Joseph even though they deplored what he did?

You got it. You may not yet have learned the old expression "Politics makes strange bedfellows," but you just saw an example of what that expression refers to.

How can you be allowed to say "Bong Hits 4 Jesus" and also "It was Adam and Eve, not Adam and Steve" in the same breath?

Welcome, once again, to the puzzle of rights in this country.

So, as you've guessed, neither side was completely happy with the court's decision. And the judges weren't happy, either. I'm not going into all of the details, which could (hint) make quite a term paper, but here's a quick rundown.

On the anti-Joseph team, Supreme Court top judge John G. Roberts Jr. argued that the principal had the right to suspend the kid because "failing to act would send a powerful message to the students" that, in effect, the school wasn't really serious about fighting drug use. (He did note that the message on the banner was "cryptic" and "gibberish," though.) Three more judges agreed with his decision, without comment, but the fifth, Justice Clarence Thomas, was moved to add that "in light of the history of public education," students (and that means you) have no right of freedom of speech in school under the First Amendment. None. Nada.

Then there was Justice Stephen G. Breyer. He didn't think that the principal should have to pay damages (1/2 vote for the principal), but he argued that the Supreme Court should have stayed away from the discussion of the First Amendment (1/2 vote for young Frederick). Might confuse things, he opined. Apparently, Judge Breyer wanted the controversy to be seen as an "authority" issue, not a "free speech" issue. It is easier to define what a school principal can legally do than to define what an American kid can legally say.

Justice John Paul Stevens, who wrote the opinion for the four (or 3 1/2) dissenting judges, was pretty funny. He argued that the majority was just making up a special free speech exception for any mention of drugs. With tongue firmly in cheek, he asked whether or not the decision would have been different if the offending banner had read, "Wine Sips 4 Jesus." That, he wrote, could be read as both pro-wine and pro-Christianity. (If you haven't heard about the Christian rite of communion, look it up.) But Stevens certainly understood the subversive message Joseph put out there; he just didn't think it was that big a deal.

So where are we?

Hard to say. All I can tell you with certainty is this: There will be more court cases, leading to more decisions that will perhaps cause even more controversy (or not) . . . There will be attempts in Congress to define the issues of the decision with new legislation . . . And the world, including me, will opine!

Most important, you—along with your friends and parents and teachers—will have to figure out how this decision affects your daily life. So, in case you ever thought Washington, D.C., was far away, think again. The Supremes are in your face, for better or worse. Even when you're trying to decide what to say or write in school, they're looking over your shoulder. You have a lot to think about . . .

Oh, one other thing . . . young Joseph Frederick, the high school student in this case, is now twenty-three years old. That says a lot. Your rights take time to define. Yes, I am a poet.

AWESOME
multiple-choice quiz no. 3

1. The Supremes are . . .
  a. Last year's winning team in the NCAA final.
  b. A girl band based in Seattle.
  c. The nine judges on the Supreme Court.
  d. The most popular drugs in downtown Chicago.

2. "Due process" is . . .
  a. Guaranteed by the Fourteenth Amendment.
  b. Too difficult for most people to understand.
  c. The legal basis for allowing kids to be paddled.
  d. What happens when the morning sun hits wet grass.

3. A 5–4 vote on the Supreme Court means that . . .
  a. There has to be a recount.
  b. A decision may well be reversed when new judges
     replace current ones.
  c. Overtime rules go into effect.
  d. Republican judges outnumber Democratic ones.

4. The ACLU is . . .

  a. The official representative of high school softball.

  b. The final answer revealed by *The Da Vinci Code*.

  c. A group that advocates rights but sometimes drives me nuts with their extremism.

  d. A club that gives an annual dinner to honor the Founding Fathers.

5. What you are allowed to wear to school is determined by . . .

  a. Your political beliefs.

  b. The local school authorities.

  c. Your parents.

  d. *Us* magazine.

And, now, the correct answers:

1. c; 2. a; 3. b; 4. c; 5. b.

6

ALL
IN THE FAMILY

urprise! In most polls, American parents name their teenager's "attitude" as the one thing that is most likely to drive them nuts.

Well, you knew that. If you're one of the culprits, your parents have undoubtedly "taken pains" to explain this concept to you.

And, just in case they're looking over your shoulder, I want to PROMISE them that I'm not writing anything in this chapter that could make you less pleasant to live with.

Is that even possible?

Just kidding.

Still, it has to be said: As a child who is legally under the care of adults, you have certain rights at home. Most of them are in the realm of common sense. Your rights entitle you to food, lodging, health care, and freedom from abuse. My guess is that you probably take all of this for granted. The government doesn't have to force your parents to respect these rights. Your parents do so because they want you to have a good life, and because they love you.

There are exceptions out there, I know. But that's when a kid needs more than a book; that's when the law needs to get involved. If you are the victim of abuse or neglect, it is your right to seek protection. See the guidance counselor at your school. Immediately!

Generally, though, most American kids are well cared for. Of course, as you get older, even if you're still legally underage, it's natural to start spreading your wings. You begin staking out "positions"!

Try these on:

—"It's my life! I can choose the friends I want! Hogtooth is really cool!"

—"I'm not a baby! NO ONE wears jeans at the waist like those nerds in your old yearbook. Hello!"

—"Mom! I know about sex, okay? Going to that new movie isn't going to turn me into a slut!"

And so forth.

KIDS ARE
AMERICANS TOO

If you keep up the attitude, you are likely to lose the argument, because the courts have pretty much agreed that your parents or legal guardians have the right to make these kinds of decisions for you. They have a right to supervise your conduct and instill in you their vision of right and wrong. Remember, even the movie theaters can keep you out of R-rated flicks until you're seventeen.

When you reach age eighteen, you can make all your own decisions about how you behave (that is, if you live outside your parents' home). But until then, your parents rule. Literally!

Sorry.

Let me confess something right here. (And you're not really going to be surprised!)

When I was your age, I was too stupid to think about my rights. I mean, for me, it was simple. When I did what my parents or the school or the church did not want me to do, I ran the risk of being punished. (And, as I mentioned in my previous book for kids your age, that could mean that my very large father might use me as a door knocker with his very large fist.)

At times, I was out of control. I didn't consider what my rights were or weren't. Most of the time, I just did what I wanted to do and tried not to become the target of an adult's wrath.

Again, I was stupid. My parents, more than many, accepted their obligations to feed, clothe, and try to educate me and my younger sister. They stood up for me when someone outside the house was unfair to me. They made me accept the blame when I did something unfair to someone else.

Me at your age.

In other words, they did a good job, most of the time. And I didn't make things easy for them. I just took their good job for granted. It took me a long, long time—much too long—to realize how hard they worked and how much I owed them. You see, I just didn't think about the whole balance (that word again) between rights and responsibilities. I was an idiot!

There's no other word for it. In my defense, my friends were pinheads as well. Maybe life was simpler then. You've heard the old story: The wife and mother stayed at home, cooking and cleaning; the father went out into the world five days a week to earn money; the children were supposed to keep out of trouble—and pick up their rooms!

Believe me, I know that your world is much more complicated than that. Maybe that's why people your age are so much smarter about rights and responsibilities. Maybe that's why you ask so many good questions and have the courage to challenge things that seem wrong to you.

But while you think about your own rights, I urge you to think about your parents' rights, too, and about how the world sometimes tries to weaken them.

PARENTS UNDER ATTACK?

Here's a situation that I reported on and summed up in my last book for adults, *Culture Warrior.* I'll be brief. Try to read it as if you were a parent, and think about what your rights would be in that case.

A few years ago, ridiculous school officials in Palmdale, California, gave a test to kids in the second through fifth grades. You know, the old standardized testing thing. Only this time, the kids were asked to tell how they felt about activities such as "thinking about touching other people's private parts."

I'm not making this up. Okay, imaginary parent, that was only one example of the type of questions these kids were asked. The others are, uh, in the same ballpark.

So what do you think? Did the school have a right to ask such questions? I'll give you a moment, then I'll tell you what the courts decided. But here's your assignment: You decide first what your reaction would be if your child was in those grades in Palmdale and was forced to take that "test."

Well, here's what happened, in summary. Some parents asked school officials to stop giving the test. The "educators" basically ignored them. The parents sued. Eventually, to cut to the chase, a federal appeals court found in favor of the school system.

That's right, imaginary parent. The judges decided that you don't have the right to prevent your young child from experiencing what the school decides is good for his or her education—even if you are outraged, horrified, or shocked by the subject matter. Explicit sex questions for seven-year-olds? Come on!

Okay, let's jump back to your house today. If you're in conflict with a parent over something the school is teaching you (or not teaching you), I don't know whether you're right or not. If you think your parent is keeping you from an activity that your friends are allowed to enjoy, then ditto . . . I still don't know who's wrong or right.

But I think I do know something important: Because they do their job, because the law backs them up (sometimes), your parents have rights that will often END THE DISCUSSION.

Aha! You see, I bet you did not agree with the Palmdale school officials . . . or with the court that backed them up. (If I'm wrong about that, I'd sure like you to e-mail me with your point of view and argument. I'll listen.)

KIDS ARE
AMERICANS TOO

But with the shoe on the other foot, maybe you can under-stand why your parents believe that their decisions about your school and your activities are part of their rights as parents. But that's another book. One you'll read about fifteen years from now.

At this point, your humble author needs a break. So let's go to the movies!

SCENE FROM MOVIE ABOUT IDIOT KID

Idiot Kid: I can come home when I want to! All the other kids can stay out till midnight!

Father: But you're not all the other kids. You're my son.

Idiot Kid: They think I'm a nerd!

Father: They are wrong.

Idiot Kid: I'm staying out! What are you going to do about it?

Father: (after a pause) That is not a smart question.

No, it is not! And that's not a smart kid, because he isn't dealing with reality. (You know, that thing they do TV shows about?)

The reality is that your parents have rights. Which leads to another movie.

SCENE FROM MOVIE ABOUT SMART KID

Smart Kid: Dad?

Father: What's up, son?

Smart Kid: I know you worry when I'm out after eleven at night.

Father: You bet I do.

Smart Kid: You worry because I might do something stupid, or because I might get hurt, right?

Father: You got it.

Smart Kid: Okay, that's your right. I understand that.

Father: (chokes on sandwich)

Smart Kid: But what if we worked something out?

Father: (regaining control) I'm . . . listening.

Smart Kid: See, the final game of the World Series, probably, because of the time difference in the West, won't be over until midnight.

Father: Is something wrong with our TV?

Smart Kid: No, but the rest of the team will be watching at Jeff's house . . . Wait; wait, please. And Jeff's father said he would stay up with us and drive home everybody who needs a ride.

Okay, I think this movie will have a happy ending.

And I think you see why. There's a happy ending for the kid's request. It's logical and well thought out—and respectful of his father's rights!

A Fine Story

For a lot of reasons—partly because I don't want to interfere with their right to privacy—I don't talk much about my two children, a daughter and a son.

There's not much to say, anyway.

They have always believed that they should try to do exactly what their mother and I tell them to do.

They have learned never to push the envelope, because I

have clearly spelled out their rights and obligations.

You will never hear a disagree—

★ ★ ★

Have you lost your mind?

If you believed any part of that, you are in need of serious help!

Yes, from the time they were born, my clever, very independent children have, well, stood up for their rights, or for the rights they wanted.

That is a good thing.

I don't want wimps in the house.

On the other hand, there are rules. Part of daily life—and I mean *daily* life—is the back-and-forth between parent and child. It's really, of course, the back-and-forth between what the parent believes to be the right thing and how the growing child wants to expand his or her horizons. Perfectly natural.

A few years ago, when my son was just learning to walk, he knew the rule of "only two cookies" after dinner. He didn't like that rule. With the ability to walk, he developed a comic routine. He would point at the TV, for example, so I would be distracted and look away, then he'd tiptoe over to the cookie jar. I would snap my head back and fix my gaze on him. He would pretend to be unaware of the jar. I would look back at the TV, he would creep closer to the jar. I'd swivel again and catch him in the act.

All during this performance, he could hardly keep from giggling, and neither could I. We both knew what the other was up to. And it was fun for both of us.

Did I let him have the wonderful third cookie? Yes. Was I letting him take the first step into a life of crime? Probably not.

Here's what I think he was doing, even at that very young age. He was pushing the envelope, but he was smart enough to know that the appropriate method was not to scream and throw a tantrum—not with me. So he tricked me—yes, I admit it—by coming up with a game that put us both in a good mood. He earned the cookie with his wit. That's how I saw it.

What does this incident have to do with you? Maybe, quite a bit.

In this little anecdote, parent and child negotiated a compromise. I expect that he and his sister will be negotiating with their mother and me for just about the rest of our lives. That's how it works.

I can tell you, or the court can tell you, that as a kid you have certain rights in the home. But you have to be smart and reasonable about getting those rights recognized. If things have been difficult in the home lately, whatever the reason, you have to step back and decide how to earn the cookie. You have to engage with your parent, not leap into a confrontation.

Alarmed by news stories about the health risks of smoking cigarettes, a fourteen-year-old boy in Arizona begs his parents to stop smoking. They try but find it too difficult. Finally, he decides that it is his "right" not to be exposed to second-hand smoke in the house, because that is thought to be dangerous to one's health as well. Will the state force his parents to stop smoking when he's around? Will they take the boy away from his family? So far, neither of those things is likely to happen in this country. Stay tuned for a possible "intervention" from the ACLU.

By now, you know that the process of dealing with this "right" could take so long that the boy would be off to college or out in the job market before the state agencies and the courts came to any sort of final, binding decision.

But that would be insane. That boy and his parents should be able to negotiate a solution without getting school, church, government, and community involved. Should the parents offer to

KIDS ARE
AMERICANS TOO

smoke only on a screened-in porch outside, following the example of many work environments and public gathering places today? That would be good, but what would the boy be contributing in return?

Negotiations work best when each side gets something and also gives something. Let's say that they work out a deal like this: The parents will offer to smoke outside if he will always use headphones when he plays his rap music. Or, they'll cut down on smoking if he turns off the computer games and exercises more. (He cares about his health, right? Aha!)

The exact terms of the agreement would depend upon the several personal factors involved. But common ground can be found in almost every family dispute over your rights as opposed to your parents' rights. (I know you'll e-mail me if you think I don't know what I'm talking about, and I'll listen. But most of the time, rights in the home can be thrashed out without involving the outside world. Think how lucky you are that you're not the daughter of Alec Baldwin and Kim Basinger. It seems to me that from the time she was six or so, they've made her life a living hell. They do NOT have the right to do that.)

The same advice should apply to your rights in the community, but the more people there are to get involved, the more complicated the situation is likely to become.

7

YOUR RIGHTS VS. THEIR RIGHTS

Where do school rights end, and community rights begin, or vice versa? Sometimes, it's really not easy to say. But here's a clue . . . When an incident at school becomes the talk of the town, and when news reporters appear on the campus lawn with their lights, cameras, and mics, then the community is on the case.

Something like that happened in a posh little community northeast of Manhattan this past spring. In fact, you probably heard about it. After all, the kids involved gave their side of the story on national TV, including NBC's *Today* show.

PROSE AND A CON?

It was all about the "V-word." Three sixteen-year-old girls at John Jay High School in Katonah-Lewisboro were told they would be suspended for a day because they used the word in front of an audience of fellow students. This group of honor students was giving a reading from a very famous play, *The Vagina Monologues,* at an evening event held by the school's literary magazine.

Were the girls deprived of their rights of free speech by this action?

Did the school have the right to suspend them because they crossed the line by using what some people think is an obscenity in public?

Before you decide, note that there are contradictory versions of the incident. (As usual.) The school charged that the girls had promised teachers before the event that they would not use the word. Doing so, in that case, seemed to officials like insubordination. It wasn't the word but the broken promise that got the girls suspended, school officials explained.

The girls alleged that they had never promised not to use the word.

In any case, the entire community didn't buy the school's explanation. While students set up a Web site protesting the suspensions (and sold supportive T-shirts), many parents in the well-educated, affluent community defended the use of the word as a perfectly legitimate anatomical term. Others disagreed, arguing that the use of the word was inappropriate since very young students could have attended the event.

And so forth . . .

My point is that the issue stirred such strong emotions that the community became involved in what was otherwise a school incident: On the one side, many parents agreed with the girls that the school was practicing censorship; on the other, many parents agreed with the school's position.

This could have been quite a mess, but everyone calmed down long enough to keep it from getting to that point. First off, the school decided not to suspend the girls until the community was given an opportunity to discuss the situation. Sounds like unusual good sense to me. Second, the school board held an open meeting to talk the whole thing out.

What word have I not used?

Right . . . *court.*

No lawyers, no lawsuits, no visits from the ACLU. Instead, the community decided that everyone should be heard and that the final decision should take into account the various points of view.

From there, the process moved quickly. The day before the open meeting, the school rescinded the suspensions. The next evening, parents and other members of the community showed up for the meeting and seemed to be, by all accounts, just about evenly split on the issue. Of course, the media were there in unusual numbers. The actor Stanley Tucci also appeared, apparently doing research for a documentary about censorship in America.

Meanwhile, teachers at the high school sent out a letter in support of the girls. Next, the New York Civil Liberties Union issued a statement in their defense.

So how did it all end? The community's school board decided to form a committee to set guidelines that would help prevent future incidents of this sort. The school board president, according to an account by reporter Marci Heppner in a local paper, the *Record-Review*, sought to end it all with a sense of balance: "The issue has given us and the community the opportunity to look closely at itself and to engage in a healthy and promising dialogue about school policy, student freedom of speech, censorship, authority, and the management of expectations regarding school-sponsored events."

The girls were not punished, both sides of the community were heard, officials apparently kept their cool . . . and the V-word was said.

In another area newspaper, the *Journal News*, reporter Diana Costello summed up the controversy this way:

> The U.S. Supreme Court has said students "do not shed their constitutional rights to freedom of speech and expression at the schoolhouse gate."
>
> Public school officials, however, may regulate student expression that substantially disrupts the

school environment or that infringes on the rights of others. Many courts have held that school officials can restrict student speech that is lewd, according to the First Amendment Center.

There you have it. If you can reconcile those two ideas in every situation that arises in your life, you're much smarter than I am. In real life, there's enough leeway there for the issues to continue to be debated all across the land.

For instance, I still think, as I said on my TV program, that the final decision not to suspend the girls was ridiculous.

For their trouble, the three girls wound up on national television, where they giggled their way irresponsibly through the controversy, then their superintendent, Robert Lichtenfeld, folded under pressure from the Civil Liberties Union and from some foolish parents.

It seems to me that the superintendent is the villain in this episode. He humiliated the principal at the school by undercutting his authority. And, if it's true that the girls did promise in advance not to say the word, then he sent a very bad message to all students in the district: It's okay to be deceitful.

Yes, the community served by John Jay High School obviously included a number of kids and adults who believed the girls were being censored. But that doesn't mean that the mouthy trio should be allowed to get away with falsifying their story. Remember, you have a right to be truthful. If you are dishonest, all of your other rights collapse. Why? Because all of the rest of us have a right for you to be truthful to us. That's the only way the whole thing can work.

Just the opposite of the John Jay affair happened in a small town in Nevada recently. When a high school literary magazine published a poem that criticized the townspeople, members of the community complained to school officials, who took the issue of the magazine out of circulation. Was this censorship? The kids thought so.

Similar things can happen to teachers, too. In a North Carolina town, drama teacher Peggy Boring was generally respected for directing student performances that won awards in state competitions.

But that changed when her production of a play called *Independence* appeared in a regional competition. It turned out that the play centered upon the efforts of a single mother to help her three unhappy daughters, one of whom was a lesbian. Although the play won seventeen out of twenty-one awards at the competition, several ministers in the community took issue with it. *Blasphemy, premarital sex, homosexuality,* and *promiscuity* were the words they used to describe its content. Although the play was not performed at the school, a section of it had been presented in one English class. A student in that class complained, prompting her parents to complain, too. The teacher was subsequently transferred to another school as punishment.

Eventually, the teacher brought a lawsuit against the school, and the case was tried in the courts, but the federal appeals court

KIDS ARE
AMERICANS TOO

threw it out by a vote of 7–6. Close call again. Seven judges felt strongly; the six on the other side felt just as strongly. As I write, the U.S. Supreme Court is deciding whether or not to hear the case.

There were many issues involved here—a teacher's arguable right to freedom from censorship, a student's arguable right not to hear or see material in class that can be perceived as offensive, the principal's arguable right to determine what students are taught—but the point is that, in a way very different from the New York story, the community got involved.

So, here's the bottom line: Your rights as a kid are sometimes going to be determined by the ideas and beliefs of the community in which you live.

You can decide to buck the tide and try to change the community. You can protest. You can get the ACLU or whomever to represent you in court.

But when the community's interest is involved, it's probably best to get everyone to calm down and negotiate.

This free-speech thing is pretty tricky. Particularly when politics is involved.

Pink, a singer you probably know something about, shocked some Americans and amused others, I guess, when she came out with a song called "Dear Mr. President." The lady does not like George Bush, his actions and policies, and maybe his pet dog. She pulled no punches.

Fine. But when Molly Shoul, ten years old, decided to perform the ditty at her elementary school's talent show in Coral Springs, Florida, the principal stepped in. By now, you know the drill. The principal said the song was too political and otherwise inappropriate for kids in grammar school. Molly's mother, a high school teacher, accused the teacher of "just running scared . . . [not wanting] to upset any parents." Molly herself noted only that the song is "really cool."

And about a year before, the same school district allowed a high school kid to sport a shirt charging that the president is an INTERNATIONAL TERRORIST. He won the right after some back-and-forth with officials, but still.

Molly was pretty flexible. She substituted a song about teenage girls competing for the love of some boy.

What does all of this mean? You tell me. But for one thing, these debates are springing up in schools all across America, and you can bet that's going to continue. You can also bet there will always be at least two sides, and two interpretations of rights. Here, what's most important? Molly's right to attack Bush in song? The principal's right to protect the other children from disturbing words? Mrs. Shoul's rights . . . the rights of the other parents (who are probably divided)?

You decide. Because, sooner or later, you're going to have to.

STICKING UP FOR OTHERS

Any kind of bullying is a bad thing. I make that point again and again on *The Factor.* I have to. The bullying stories come in from all across the country like a weekly tsunami. I mean it.

So wouldn't it be a good thing if a kid in East Hartford, Connecticut, writes a letter to the school newspaper that exposes bullying?

Well, maybe, but the school principal wouldn't let the letter be printed.

This quote from the student's letter may offer a clue to what irked the principal:

> Why is the staff so bent on us wearing I.D.'s and not swearing, but when they hear someone getting ranked on they have nothing to say?

You got it. The principal didn't like the idea that the letter supposedly suggested, in his words, "that all the teachers look the other way."

Oh, and he also said the paper has a policy against printing letters that are unsigned.

See, the kid who wrote it wanted to remain anonymous. He was afraid that he would be (I know! You guessed it!) bullied because of it.

You can see that I think the principal is a pinhead. But, and here is the point, school administrators can almost always exercise their right to keep something they don't like out of a school-sponsored publication.

End of story?

No way. Several students were inspired to make an end run around their principal by sending letters, signed and unsigned, to the local newspaper, the *Journal Inquirer*. So, what could have been a discussion on campus sparked by a letter to the school newspaper turned into a big controversy that got the attention of the whole community.

Good for you, kids.

Not too smart, principal.

You draw your own conclusions here, but there are times when it's not a good idea to claim a right—in this case, the school's right to censor the newspaper—if someone else is going to be sharp enough to figure out how to exercise their rights. I think the students won a scuffle that did not have to take place.

FREEDOM OF THE PRESS?

I hate to say it, but sometimes your rights are going to be ignored in the strangest places. Suppose you're a senior girl in high school who wins a national contest because you write really good news articles. Pretty cool, right? Then suppose a group of women journalists brings you to a luncheon at a fine hotel in New York City where you and other winners will be honored. Then suppose that Rosie O'Donnell is the guest speaker and she makes the air purple with nasty language that is not allowed in ANY legitimate newspaper.

Well, stop supposing. That actually happened recently. What did the professional journalists say? That the award-winning girls were getting a dose of "reality." I think those young ladies had the right not to hear such trash. I think the whole thing was insulting. But their "role models" just laughed. Not good, kid.

ASK
O'REILLY!
(A Special Feature)

O'Reilly: Have you read all of the court decisions represented in this book so far?

You: Is this a test?

O'Reilly: No.

You: Yes.

O'Reilly: (laughs) Okay. Not a test, but I have a question.

You: I knew it.

O'Reilly: Just hold on . . . Have you agreed with every court decision?

You: Every one of them?

O'Reilly: Yes.

You: No.

O'Reilly: (laughs) Would anyone?

You: Probably not.

O'Reilly: You got it. But . . . the United States is a nation of laws made by courts and elected officials. Even if we disagree, we must obey them, or suffer the consequences. Not to obey the laws would lead to anarchy (great word). And no one's rights are respected when there's anarchy.

You: I might be getting a headache.

O'Reilly: Deal with it.

(Okay, okay . . . If you're not going to look it up, *anarchy* means something like "chaos" or "mob rule." You really don't want that. Ask the people you see running for their lives in certain countries on the news programs.)

ARE RIGHTS ALWAYS GOOD FOR YOU?

"Of course!" you might cry. "The more rights, the better!"

Let's see about that . . .

Ten years ago, my friend Sally B. was a seventeen-year-old living in a western state. She was the kind of cheerful, energetic young woman who is often called "life-loving." I'm happy to say that she is "life-loving" again.

You caught that word *again*.

There's something that none of us—not her family, not her friends, not her teachers and priest—knew about Sally a decade ago, but it explains why she went on a downward slide that included drugs, alcohol, self-destructive behavior, depression, and self-hatred for years and years. Perhaps, just perhaps, her home state gave Sally more rights than she could handle.

It began with a stupid act made worse by bad luck. Sally got drunk one night and had sex with her boyfriend for the first time. She got pregnant. That may sound hard to believe, but I know her, and she wouldn't lie about this. Reeling out of her mind from the shock, she didn't tell anyone, not her boyfriend, not her parents or any of her friends. It was guilt, pure and simple. She was not afraid that her parents would scream at her or reject her. Far from it. She was afraid that they would be hurt, perhaps ashamed. Although she was under eighteen years old at the time and living at home with her parents, she could legally get an abortion in her state without notifying her mother and father. And so she did.

Now, notice that in most states today, she would not have had that option at her age. Parental consent would have been required by law. And you could argue that such a rule actually respects the parents' rights in circumstances like Sally's. Each state makes its own rules about underage abortion. Some states support parental rights more strongly than others do.

Let me simply report that the rights extended to Sally in her state left her free to keep her secret from virtually everyone in her life except Planned Parenthood and the physician who performed the abortion. She was too ashamed to confide in any of her friends. The result? Sally believes that the guilt and shame she felt sent her spiraling through almost a decade of misery, despite countless hours of therapy. The abortion, she thinks today, was directly responsible for her crippling unhappiness and acts of self-destruction. But, had she lived across a state line, the story could have been completely different.

Let me be clear, I'm not specifically entering into the abortion fray here. I'm only suggesting that sometimes, a right that looks pretty good on the surface might give us more independence than we can handle. And by "we," I certainly include adults. (I won't believe you if you tell me that you can't think of at least one adult who has more independence than he or she can handle. And I'm not even thinking of Snoop Dogg.)

Even when it all started, Sally felt that the whole thing was more than she could manage by herself. But the state didn't force her to tell her parents, and she couldn't emotionally force herself to do so.

I'm just saying, okay? Sometimes, rules are better for us than extended rights. Sometimes.

And isn't it amazing that what happens in one person's life during a crisis can depend so heavily upon what state lines he or she lives within? Worth thinking about?

I'm just saying . . .

8

GOTTA KEEP THINKING ABOUT THESE THINGS

As you've noticed by now, this is not the kind of book that provides lists of rights and restrictions. What I've been trying to do, in many different ways, is explain the process involved in sensibly exercising and protecting your rights.

There are books in the marketplace that offer detailed answers to such questions as "Do I lose any rights if I'm underage and pregnant?" or "If my parents get a divorce, will I still get to visit my grandparents?"

These questions are just two among ninety-five that appear in *What Are My Rights?*, a handy little paperback by attorney and former judge Thomas A. Jacobs. You might want to page through his book and others like it when you are facing a specific set of issues.

But here, I mean to keep talking about the big picture. (Remember? We don't sweat the small stuff.)

CAREFUL WHAT YOU ASK FOR

If you know any lawyers, you probably already know that they often try to avoid having a judge or jury make a decision. (Remember Patrick's dispute over the yearbook photo?)

Why? Because court decisions aren't very predictable. Sure, you think you are right in a dispute. So does the other side. Since very few disputes in life have a slam-dunk ending, there's always the possibility that even reasonable people will disagree with your side of things. And what about unreasonable people? Well, let's not even think about them.

So, no matter how strongly you feel about your rights (or what you think your rights are), it's probably smart to resolve things outside the courts . . . if you can, while also sticking to your beliefs. Basically, I'm suggesting that you pick and choose your legal battles carefully.

Still, there are times when you really don't have a choice.

As we near the end of this book I hope you agree that this has been an informative and fun trip we've taken together. What I've tried to do throughout is get you interested in how your rights were developed in this country and are still being fought, challenged, developed, and maintained today. I want you to become a part of that process. I want you to think for yourself, but always understand that your rights have to be in harmony with the rights of others.

Now, the ACLU may come after me for referring to religion, but here goes: I believe the best place to start, before you decide whether your rights are being recognized or not, may be with the Golden Rule.

Do unto others as you would have them do unto you. Yeah, another idea in old-fashioned language, but the idea itself still works today.

I like the stories we've looked at where people calmed down, listened to one another, and found a compromise. I don't like the ones that resulted in court cases that dragged on for years, close court decisions that didn't really make anyone happy, insulting comments from both sides in the news media, and all the rest of the noisemaking that leaves everyone tired and disgusted at the end of the day.

Respect for one another's rights should not drive wedges between us. It should unite us. Let's all try to understand *and live* by that ideal.

ASK
O'REILLY!
(A Special Feature)

O'Reilly: Suppose I gave you a *Bill O'Reilly Factor* T-shirt?

You: Cool!

O'Reilly: Would you wear it to your school?

You: Sure!

O'Reilly: But . . . could you?

You: Why not? . . . Oh, I see. Dress code?

O'Reilly: Exactly.

You: Well, I really wouldn't be making a political statement. Just being a fan.

O'Reilly: But a fan of what? I mean, some of your

classmates—and they would be wrong!—might think that I'm an obnoxious blowhard. And that *The Factor* is not a good concept.

You: Naw.

O'Reilly: They might have read that charge, and worse, in print or on some nutty Web site. They might agree.

You: So? I disagree.

O'Reilly: Exactly. And what does your school think about that?

You: They can't tell me what to think.

O'Reilly: No, they can't. But they can decide that wearing an O'Reilly T-shirt would upset other people. You and those other people might argue about it or you might just smirk at one another or stare one another down. And the phrase for that is . . .

You: *Distraction from the educational process.*

O'Reilly: Hey, you *have* been listening.

you: We're talking about my life, right?

O'Reilly: Get this. Early in 2007, a fourteen-year-old girl was punished by her middle school in Northern California for wearing kneesocks decorated with an image of Tigger.

you: From the cartoon *Winnie-the-Pooh*?

O'Reilly: It was a book first. Sorry, had to say that.

you: Okay, okay.

O'Reilly: The school argues that Tigger, whose politics are not known to me (or to anyone else), violated their Appropriate Attire Policy.

you: You're kidding me.

O'Reilly: (shakes head)

you: You're not kidding me. And there's going to be a lawsuit?

O'Reilly: Right.

You: And this will go on for some time, and lawyers are involved, and the ACLU has weighed in?

O'Reilly: Right, again.

You: Oh, brother.

O'Reilly: As usual, there are all kinds of complications. It turns out that the policy was set up to keep kids from wearing gang symbols or sexy images and sayings. It also turns out that the girl has been punished twelve times for wearing clothing with decorations that the school found inappropriate.

You: You mean, she's been pushing it.

O'Reilly: Maybe. But this is what I have to ask . . . Was the Constitution written by Ben and Tom and the rest of our Founding Fathers so that she could wear a fictional animal to the classroom?

You: I don't think the answer is easy.

O'Reilly: Yes, you've been listening, all right. What size T-shirt do you wear?

FINAL AWESOME
multiple-choice quiz

1. The First Amendment guarantees that you can . . .
   a. Express your opinion frankly when asked in school.
   b. Interrupt a fellow student who disagrees with you.
   c. Wear the symbols of your religion openly at school.
   d. Criticize school policies in the school newspaper.

2. The authorities can legally intervene at your home if your parents . . .
   a. Do not feed and clothe you properly.
   b. Prevent you from watching TV.
   c. Insist that you go with them to church.
   d. Take away your cell phone when your grades fall.

3. Most lawsuits against schools occur because . . .
   a. Lawyers will do anything to make money.
   b. Administrators do not clearly explain their rules to the community.
   c. Parents want their kids to be independent.
   d. Opposing sides do not calmly negotiate an agreement.

4. **The Supreme Court decisions of your future will be most affected by . . .**
   a. Increased government funding for better legal training.
   b. The politicians you and your generation elect to office.
   c. An increase in the number of judges from minority groups.
   d. The opinions of anchorpersons at Fox, CBS, and ABC.

5. **You are now a better person because you . . .**
   a. Just watched a rerun of *The O.C.*
   b. Have applied for membership in the ACLU.
   c. Read my book and plan to tell other kids about it.
   d. Believe everything that Dr. Phil says.

The correct answers:

1. a; 2. a; 3. d; 4. b; 5. c.

EXTRA CREDIT

To win arguments, or to help you understand what's behind breaking news stories, or to research school assignments, here are the ten amendments that make up the Bill of Rights, speaking for themselves . . .

Do you need to know this stuff?

I don't see why not. You're an American too!

If you've learned from this book that your daily life is now—and will always be—deeply affected by laws . . . AND by the people who make them or interpret them, then why not take a few minutes to see how it all began?

So here is a quick look at the Bill of Rights. Of course, I've added some pithy comments. (That's my job!)

If you disagree, or your parent or teacher disagrees, you know where to find me.

1. FREEDOM OF SPEECH, PRESS, RELIGION, AND PETITION

Congress shall make no law respecting an establishment of religion, or prohibiting the free exercise thereof; or abridging the freedom of speech, or of the press; or the right of the people peaceably to assemble, and to petition the Government for a redress of grievances.

O'Reilly Pith: The tricky phrase here is "no law respecting an establishment of religion." Sensibly enough, it's known in the trade as the "establishment clause."

Most of the wrangling based on this amendment hinges on the different possible interpretations of this clause. Yes, it's there to separate church and state, but exactly how? At the very least it means that the government can't establish a national religion, financially support a religion, or show preference for one religion over another or for religion over irreligious philosophies. But more precise questions than those have been raised over the years. For instance, does it violate this clause to have a military chaplain present for the sake of our wounded soldiers overseas? And if that's true, wouldn't the absence of a military chaplain violate another right—our soldiers' right to free exercise of religion? Can the grant of monies to a hospital serving people of all denominations be construed as showing preference for one religion over another when the hospital is owned and operated by the Roman Catholic Church? And what about when a public school gives students time off for the observance of a religious holiday? (I *know* you have feelings about *that* issue!) These are the kinds of questions that have already been hotly debated. Many more continue to be debated every day. So have fun out there! These arguments are likely to continue as long as America lasts.

2. RIGHT TO KEEP AND BEAR ARMS

A well-regulated militia, being necessary to the security of a free State, the right of the people to keep and bear arms, shall not be infringed.

O'Reilly Pith: Here, the pesky phrase is "well-regulated militia." You have no idea, I'd bet, how antigun lobbyists, including the ACLU, can take that phrase out for a walk around the block and knock it senseless. Anyway, you'll have to deal with the potential for misinterpretation right there. Does this amendment protect the right for an individual to bear arms for his or her own self-protection? Or does it mean only the militia can possess guns? You see how polarized the argument can get. Good luck arguing that one without coming to blows!

3. CONDITIONS FOR QUARTERS OF SOLDIERS

No soldier shall, in time of peace be quartered in any house, without the consent of the owner, nor in time of war, but in a manner to be prescribed by law.

O'Reilly Pith: Are you worried that a squad of Marines is going to be installed in your house, taking over the TV remotes? No, you are not. But it used to happen, before that Philadelphia meeting and before George Washington and the guys defeated the British Redcoats, who *did* kick people out of their homes. So sit back and relax, you've got the whole place to yourself, kid.

4. RIGHT OF SEARCH AND SEIZURE REGULATED

The right of the people to be secure in their persons, houses, papers, and effects, against unreasonable searches and seizures, shall not be violated, and no warrants shall issue, but upon probable cause, supported by oath or affirmation, and particularly describing the place to be searched, and the persons or things to be seized.

O'Reilly Pith: Okay, we've already talked about this amendment, but we have not ended the discussion by far. It continues this very day in various courts all over the land. Columnists are railing, politicians are venting, and the ACLU is collecting money—all because life is getting very, very complicated, especially with the terrorism component added into the mix. New laws and court decisions will appear; then they will be analyzed to see whether or not they actually fulfill the intent of Tom, Ben, and the rest. Stay tuned . . .

5. PROVISIONS CONCERNING PROSECUTION

No person shall be held to answer for a capital, or otherwise infamous crime, unless on a presentment or indictment of a Grand Jury, except in cases arising in the land or naval forces, or in the militia, when in actual service in time of war or public danger; nor shall any person be subject for the same offense to be twice put in jeopardy of life or limb; nor shall be compelled in any criminal case to be a witness against himself, nor be deprived of life, liberty, or property, without due process of law; nor shall private property be taken for public use without just compensation.

O'Reilly Pith: Yeah, this one is quite a mouthful. You can probably forget the military stuff for right now and concentrate on (1) the rule that a grand jury must return an indictment, (2) the provision against "double jeopardy," (3) the essential concept of "due process," and (4) the rule for compensation for your property taken by the government.

Each of these ideas is still being argued, as you know if you read newspapers, watch TV, or listen to radio . . . or hear one of your friends complain about unfair treatment of suspected criminals. And remember, Americans are entitled to these rights. But are terrorists captured in Afghanistan entitled to them? I say no. Others disagree. And we all keep talking!

6. RIGHT TO A SPEEDY TRIAL, WITNESSES, ETC.

In all criminal prosecutions, the accused shall enjoy the right to a speedy and public trial, by an impartial jury of the State and district wherein the crime shall have been committed, which district shall have been previously ascertained by law, and to be informed of the nature and cause of the accusation; to be confronted with the witnesses against him; to have compulsory process for obtaining witnesses in his favor, and to have the assistance of counsel for his defense.

KIDS ARE
AMERICANS TOO

O'Reilly Pith: Here again, the basic ideas seem to be clear enough . . . and here again, the arguments get hot. What is a "speedy" trial? What is a "public" trial? Sound obvious? Well, is a trial "public" if it's not on television? (There was no HDTV available back there in Philadelphia.) The states (remember them?) don't agree on that one yet.

What is an "impartial" jury? For example, does gender, or occupation, or racial background cause a juror to be unfair? These questions don't get the same answers from everyone involved in the law, let me tell you. What is required by the phrase "assistance of counsel"? Does that mean the court-appointed lawyer must be a Harvard graduate, or would it be fair for her to come from some lesser institution like Yale? (Sorry, kid. You know I have to say that because I hold a Harvard degree.)

7. RIGHT TO A TRIAL BY JURY

In suits at common law, where the value in controversy shall exceed twenty dollars, the right of trial by jury shall be preserved, and no fact tried by a jury shall be otherwise reexamined in any court of the United States, than according to the rules of the common law.

O'Reilly Pith: Forget the twenty-dollar rule. Half your classmates would be demanding jury trials because someone took their old running shoes or neglected to return some borrowed CDs, right? The courts have agreed on the "intent" of this clause. The more important principle here, of course, is that a case, once decided by a jury, cannot be retried elsewhere.

8. EXCESSIVE BAIL, CRUEL PUNISHMENT

Excessive bail shall not be required, nor excessive fines imposed, nor cruel and unusual punishments inflicted.

O'Reilly Pith: I'm sure you see the problems here. Define *excessive*, please. And once you've got that little chore out of the way, reel off a quick, solid definition of "cruel and unusual punishments." Does that phrase cover the death penalty? Well, unless you've been living in the basement of a mall for the last few years, you certainly know that both sides of that issue disagree about its true meaning. Once again, the debate goes on. Each side, in this case, believes it somehow knows the "intent" of the Philadelphia guys. Can each side be right? (No.) Is this a matter of life and death? (Uh . . . yes.)

KIDS ARE
AMERICANS TOO

9. RULE OF CONSTRUCTION OF CONSTITUTION

The enumeration in the Constitution, of certain rights, shall not be construed to deny or disparage others retained by the people.

O'Reilly Pith: In other words, just because they didn't mention a specific right doesn't mean it's not there. Bring on the iPods (and the lawyers)! Isn't that really what this book is about?

10. RIGHTS OF THE STATES UNDER CONSTITUTION

The powers not delegated to the United States by the Constitution, nor prohibited by it to the States, are reserved to the States respectively, or to the people.

O'Reilly Pith: By now, you see what this means. If Ben, Tom, and their friends did not give a specific right to the national government or say that the states could NOT have it, then either the states or we ourselves—you and I and everybody else in America—have that right. I believe you know that's never going to be as simple as it sounds. (You sure you don't want to go to law school? We may need you!)

You: Now, do I know everything about my rights?

O'Reilly: No.

You: When will I?

O'Reilly: Never.

You: (sigh)

O'Reilly: Look, what's true today will not be true tomorrow. The players keep changing. Ideas keep changing. Who knows what new toy your kids will have someday that will drive their teachers nuts? The rules have to change with the times.

You: Like, I mean, chaos.

O'Reilly: No, no, not chaos. The good ship Constitution stays afloat, no matter what. You have to believe that.

You: Well, I think now I do.

O'Reilly: Okay, but it doesn't steer itself. You and all of your kid friends have to keep it on course. It adjusts to the weather, the heaving seas, but smart people have to take turns at the helm.

You: Are you running for office?

O'Reilly: (laughs) No, but I want you kids to run for office someday, and support candidates, and stay involved in this rights business for the rest of your lives. You have to join the line that goes back to Ben and Tom.

You: I'll think about it.

O'Reilly: You do that.

(You and I shake hands firmly.)

THE LAST WORD

Congratulations!

You've completed a book that should help you become a better American. And the country needs you. That's right . . . the country needs you.

During my trip to Iraq in December 2006, I met hundreds of American military people ages eighteen to twenty-five. They are young adults, as you will be in a very short time. They are sacrificing greatly, trying to bring freedom and "rights" to oppressed people.

I really respect those young Americans.

Like millions of other Americans before them, our military people are willing to die so that strangers can have the right to freedom. How noble is that? And how powerful is the right to freedom?

So, when thinking about your rights as a kid, please think about our military people. They are the direct successors of Ben,

Tom, and all the rest who have kept focused on the "rights" thing throughout the history that gave you the life you have now. These young people in uniform today should make you proud. And so should your unique country, which stands for freedom throughout the world.

Thanks for reading this book, kid.

I wish you a great life.

DEFENSE SAVVY
A BRIEF GUIDE TO TERMS

Competing rights

A student you know has the right to privacy, like all the rest of us. You have the right to protect yourself from being harmed, like all the rest of us. Has he hidden a loaded pistol in his school locker? For the school to search the locker without his permission, your right to life outweighs his right to privacy. Each right is golden in itself, but sometimes they have to be weighed against each other for the greatest possible good.

Due process

The rules! You have the right to be protected from a government that would arrest, try, and convict you unfairly. Your rights to fairness at every step of the process are guaranteed. Tom, Ben, and the rest believed that human beings with power can't always be trusted. They knew from experience. A judge who can be bribed? A prosecutor who will convict an innocent person in order to further his political ambitions? A rogue cop who might "plant" evidence? These things happen. The Philadelphia guys knew it. But they also knew that laws and procedures could be set down in clear English so that good people could try to follow them.

Original intent

That's what the writers of the Constitution were actually thinking back then . . . or would be thinking if they knew about video surveillance and DNA testing and all the rest of the developments in our century. Is it possible to know for sure what they would have been thinking? Well, no. Not exactly. But we all have to work at it, or the system falls apart.

Parental obligation

This is what you have the right to expect from your parent(s) or legal guardian(s), as defined by your state. Of course, they're not supposed to harm you and they're required to take care of your needs, as long as you're a minor. Even so, some courts have found gray areas here.

Probable cause

This is a concrete reason to suspect that you're guilty of something. If someone else's missing iPod falls out of your jacket pocket, it's "probable" that you stole it. That's not proof, but it's reason enough for the authorities to search your person and otherwise pursue the truth. Same idea with the scent of marijuana on your clothes, or an open bottle of vodka visible through your car window.

Reasonable suspicion

A lesser standard than probable cause, this right is given to your school authorities by your state in order to protect the students in their care. In other words, as we talked about earlier, they can search your locker without "probable cause" but with "reasonable suspicion." For a more precise definition of this term, many a lawsuit has been taken to the courts. (You are not surprised.)

How you can

Get in Touch with Me

E-mail: O'Reilly@foxnews.com

snail mail: Bill O'Reilly

c/o HarperCollins

10 E. 53rd Street

7th floor

New York, NY 10022-5299